R. Albert Mohler, Jr.

Acts 13–28

The Church Multiplies

GOOD BOOK GUIDE

8-Session Bible Study

Acts 13-28 For You

These studies are adapted from *Acts 13–28 For You*. If you are reading *Acts 13–28 For You* alongside this Good Book Guide, here is how the studies in this booklet link to the chapters of *Acts 13–28 For You*:

Study One > Ch 1
Study Two > Ch 2-3
Study Three > Ch 3-4
Study Four > Ch 5-6
Study Five > Ch 6-7
Study Six > Ch 8-9
Study Seven > Ch 9-11
Study Eight > Ch 12

Find out more about *Acts 13–28 For You* at:
www.thegoodbook.com/for-you

Acts 13–28: The Church Multiplies
A Good Book Guide

This edition printed 2025.

Published by The Good Book Company

thegoodbook.com | thegoodbook.co.uk
thegoodbook.com.au | thegoodbook.co.nz

A CIP catalogue record for this book is available from the British Library.

Design by André Parker and Drew McCall

ISBN: 9781802541540 | JOB-008395 | Printed in India

Contents

Introduction

One of the Bible writers described God's word as "a lamp for my feet, a light on my path" (Psalm 119:105, NIV). God gave us the Bible to tell us about who he is and what he wants for us. He speaks through it by his Spirit and lights our way through life.

That means that we need to look carefully at the Bible and uncover its meaning—but we also need to apply what we've discovered to our lives.

Good Book Guides are designed to help you do just that. The sessions in this book are interactive and easy to lead. They're perfect for use in groups or for personal study.

Let's take a look at what is included in each session.

Talkabout: Every session starts with an ice-breaker question, designed to get people talking around a subject that links to the Bible study.

Investigate: These questions help you explore what the passage is about.

Apply: These questions are designed to get you thinking practically: what does this Bible teaching mean for you and your church?

Explore More: These optional sections help you to go deeper or to explore another part of the Bible which connects with the main passage.

Getting Personal: These sections are a chance for personal reflection. Some groups may feel comfortable discussing these, but you may prefer to look at them quietly as individuals instead—or leave them out.

Pray: Here, you're invited to pray in the light of the truths and challenges you've seen in the study.

Each session is also designed to be easily split into two! Watch out for the **Apply** section that comes halfway through, and stop there if you haven't got time to do the whole thing in one go.

In the back of the book, you'll find a **Leader's Guide**, which provides helpful notes on every question, along with everything else that group leaders need in order to facilitate a great session and help the group uncover the riches of God's light-giving word.

Why Study Acts 13 – 28?

In Acts 1:8 Jesus said to his disciples...

> *But you will receive power when the Holy Spirit has come upon you, and you will be my witnesses in Jerusalem and in all Judea and Samaria, and to the end of the earth.*

The church's obedience to our Lord's command is dramatically revealed in this second half of Acts.

Chapters 1 – 12 chronicled the birth and growth of the Jerusalem church, from Jesus' ascension and the coming of the Spirit at Pentecost to the martyrdom of Stephen and the conversion of Saul, and finally to the coming of the gospel to the first non-Jews. Now, chapters 13 – 28 recount how the gospel began to extend to the ends of the earth. We travel with Saul (now called Paul) throughout the Roman Empire as he preaches the gospel, plants churches, and then is arrested and put on trial for his faithfulness to Christ.

Discipleship means difficulty—a life of ease, comfort, and prosperity does not await people zealous for God's kingdom. Yet Acts also reveals the glorious grace, mercy, and power of God. When Paul faced what seemed like certain death, he pressed on with an unspeakable joy, knowing that he lived as a citizen of heaven. Paul lived zealously, relied upon the Spirit, trusted in the promises of God—and changed the world.

But the book of Acts is not only the story of the apostles and the earliest churches. It is also the story of the worldwide church: a story that now continues in your church.

These eight studies will reveal what every Christian needs as we go out as ambassadors for Christ. May God make us more zealous for his kingdom, show us our need for his Holy Spirit, and help us to trust him as we face trials and suffering in the cause of the gospel. May he encourage, strengthen, and equip us to be witnesses of Jesus Christ wherever and whoever we are: even to the end of the earth.

Creation

- Fall
- Noah
- Abraham
- Joseph
- Exodus from Egypt
- Israel reaches promised land
- King David
- Kingdom divided (Judah/Israel)
- Israel exiled
- Judah exiled
- Judah returns
- Jesus Christ
- Pentecost
- Jerusalem destroyed
- Revelation written
- Now

Jesus' return
New creation

GOOD BOOK GUIDE — BIBLE TIMELINE

Acts c. 35-60 AD

- c. 35 — Paul converted
- c. 48 — Paul's first journey
- c. 50 — Council at Jerusalem
- c. 50-52 — Paul's second journey
- c. 53-57 — Paul's third journey
- c. 58 — Paul arrested in Jerusalem
- c. 60 — Paul reaches Rome

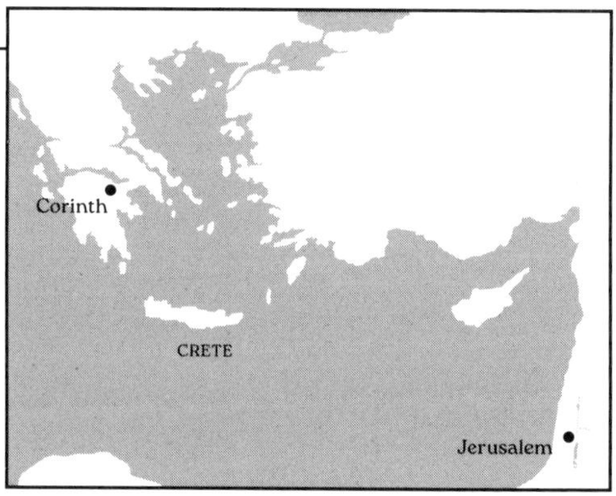

1

Mission Commenced

Acts 13:1 - 14:28

Talkabout

1. Think of a time when you have had good news to share. What responses did people have?

- How would it have felt if they simply hadn't believed you?

Investigate

📖 **Read Acts 13:1-12**

DICTIONARY

Prophet (v 1): God's messenger.
Tetrarch (v 1): a Jewish ruler under the Romans.
Fasting (v 2): going without food.
Proconsul (v 7): important Roman official.

2. What starts Saul and Barnabas off on their missionary journey?

3. What is the missionaries' strategy to begin with (v 5-6)?

4. Trace the responses of the proconsul and the magician through the passage.

Apply

5. Consider how we see God working and how he uses people in this first part of Paul and Barnabas' mission. In what ways might this affect how we think about and do evangelism ourselves?

Investigate

📖 **Read Acts 13:13-52**

DICTIONARY

Sabbath (v 14): Saturday, a holy day for Jews.
The Law and the Prophets (v 15): the Old Testament.
I have begotten (v 33): I am the father of.
Corruption (v 34): the rotting of a dead body.
Devout (v 43): pious, committed.
Reviling (v 45): rejecting.
Gentiles (v 46): non-Jews.

6. What is Paul's concluding message (v 38-41)? How do you think you would have felt to hear it?

Explore More | OPTIONAL

- Look more carefully at the rest of Paul's sermon. Can you map out his argument? Try dividing it as follows:
  - verses 16-22
  - verses 23-25
  - verses 26-27
  - verses 28-37

In verse 46, Luke records a watershed moment in the Acts narrative. The gospel will now advance to the non-Jewish world. In verse 47, Paul establishes his mission in the prophetic witness of Isaiah 49:6; it was always God's plan to send Paul to the Gentiles.

7. After the gospel is preached, who feels joy, and why?

Getting Personal | OPTIONAL

Paul reveals the significance of our response to the gospel. Why do Christians sometimes leave out the need to respond when they talk about their faith with others? When you share your faith, how can you call people to respond?

Read Acts 14:1-7

DICTIONARY

Signs and wonders (v 3): miracles.
Apostles (v 4): disciples sent by Jesus as his representatives.
Stone (v 5): attack and kill by throwing rocks.

8. What patterns do you notice in the way the gospel is preached and received? Try comparing these verses with 13:1-12, 48-52.

Read Acts 14:8-20

DICTIONARY

Zeus (v 12): king of the Greek gods.
Hermes (v 12): Greek messenger god.
Vain (v 15): empty, pointless.
Tribulations (v 22): suffering.

9. What is different about what happens in Lystra, and what remains the same?

10. How would you sum up all that has happened to Paul and Barnabas so far in these two chapters?

📖 **Read Acts 14:21-28**

DICTIONARY

Pisidia, Pamphylia (v 24): regions in modern-day Turkey.

11. How do Paul and Barnabas themselves sum up their mission (v 27)?

Apply

12. How do these chapters encourage us to keep on sharing the truth about Jesus?

- How can we help each other to remember these encouragements?

Getting Personal | OPTIONAL

Choose the aspect of the mission of Paul and Barnabas that has most struck you.

What would following their example in that aspect look like in your own life this week?

Pray

Spend time worshiping and praising God, like the disciples in 13:2.

Pray for one another, that the Spirit might equip you to go out and present the gospel faithfully and to take joy from serving the Lord in this way.

Pray for someone you would like to share the gospel with this week. Ask that, like the proconsul in 13:12, they might be "astonished at the teaching of the Lord," and that, like the Gentiles in 13:48, they might believe, rejoice in, and glorify the word of the Lord.

2

The Council in Jerusalem

Acts 15:1 - 16:5

The Story So Far...

Sent by God, Paul took the gospel into the Gentile world. Some believed and others were hostile, but the missionaries returned rejoicing at all God had done.

Talkabout

1. People have conflicts and disagreements about all kinds of things. Which are worth fighting over, and which aren't? Why do we find it hard to remember which is which?

Investigate

📖 **Read Acts 15:1-5**

DICTIONARY

Circumcise (v 1): cut off the foreskin as a religious rite.

Dissension (v 2): disagreement.
Elders (v 2): church leaders.

2. What does Luke tell us about the people in verses 1 and 5?

These teachers view Gentiles as ceremonially unclean—unacceptable to God. They think that in order to be saved, they need to be circumcised as part of obeying the Law of Moses. They have a legitimate theological concern, but they have come to the wrong conclusion.

Read Acts 15:6-12

DICTIONARY

Yoke (v 10): here, a heavy load.

Fathers (v 10): here, ancestors.

3. What does Peter say about being cleansed (v 8-9)?

4. What other reasons does he give for not imposing obedience to the Law of Moses on the Gentiles?

Explore More | OPTIONAL

The false teachers believe that the law provides a cleansing power that the gospel does not. But in verse 10 Peter points out that no one was ever able to obey the Law of Moses. The truth is that it never had the power to cleanse and make righteous. Paul explains this in his epistle to the Romans.

Read Romans 3:20-25

- What is it that brings righteousness?

Read Romans 4:3, 9-12

- Why is it incorrect to say that circumcision is necessary to be saved?
- What then was the purpose of circumcision (v 11-12)?

Read Acts 15:13-21

DICTIONARY

David (v 16): the great Old Testament king.
Remnant (v 17): remaining people.
Abstain from (v 20): avoid.
Idols (v 20): false gods.

5. In verses 15-18, what argument does James add?

In verses 19-21, James sets out moral instructions for the Gentiles to observe. He has in mind the levitical commands and laws that Jews thought were particularly important and necessary. Gentiles should avoid the things that Jews view with the highest disgust and revulsion.

6. What do you think is James' motivation here?

Getting Personal | OPTIONAL

Sound theology should usher believers' hearts into greater worship of God, strengthening and encouraging the faith of the body.

Do you know any Christians who need encouragement? What truth do they need to be reminded of?

Apply

7. Is there anything in our churches that could give the wrong impression to non-Christians about the importance of the way we act?

Investigate

Read Acts 15:22-35

DICTIONARY

One accord (v 25): agreement.

8. If you had been a Gentile believer in Antioch, how would you have been encouraged as you received the news from Jerusalem?

Read Acts 15:36-41

John Mark had accompanied Paul and Barnabas on their first missionary journey (13:5). As that mission turned toward Gentile lands, however, Mark deserted the company (v 13). Now, two years or so later, Barnabas wants to bring Mark along on their second missionary journey. This becomes a cause of division.

9. What motivates Paul? What do you think motivates Barnabas?

- Do you think they disagree well?

📖 **Read Acts 16:1-5**

DICTIONARY

Observance (v 4): obedience.

Given the agreement by the Jerusalem Council that circumcision is not necessary for salvation, it may surprise us that Paul circumcises Timothy here in verse 3.

10. Why do you think Paul feels it is important to circumcise Timothy?

Explore More | OPTIONAL

Paul explains his attitude in 1 Corinthians 8 – 10, saying that we should humbly submit ourselves and our preferences to the needs of others.

📖 **Read 1 Corinthians 8:4-13**

- How does an attitude like Paul's help believers?

📖 **Read 1 Corinthians 9:19-23**

- How does it advance the gospel?

Getting Personal | OPTIONAL

What would it look like for you to surrender your rights or personal preferences…

- for the sake of Christians?
- for the sake of non-Christians?

Apply

11. What divides Christians today? How can we strengthen the church in the face of this? Think about how this applies to your church specifically.

Pray

Pray for yourself: Pause to reflect on the ways in which you have fallen short of the holiness of God this week, and then on the grace of the Lord Jesus, who, by his blood, has cleansed the hearts of all those who believe.

Pray for one another: Pray that you would have both the theological conviction of Peter and the humility of Timothy.

Pray for the church: Based on your answers to question 11, pray for the strengthening of the worldwide church and of your own church.

3

The World Upside Down

Acts 16:6 - 17:34

The Story So Far...

Sent by God, Paul took the gospel into the Gentile world. Some believed and others were hostile, but the missionaries returned rejoicing at all God had done.

False teachers threatened the true gospel by rejecting Gentile converts, but a council sought to unite believers around the truth.

Talkabout

1. How diverse are the people you know? How do their backgrounds or values influence the way you relate to them?

Investigate

📖 **Read Acts 16:6-15**

DICTIONARY

Phrygia, Galatia, Asia, Mysia, Bithynia (v 6-7): regions in modern-day Turkey.

Macedonia (v 9): then, a region of modern-day northern Greece.

Prevailed upon (v 15): persuaded.

Did you spot the change from *they* to *we*? Luke is telling us that he himself joined Paul's missionary party at this point. He does not tag along as a disinterested journalist or historian but serves as a member of the team, called to preach the gospel.

2. How do we see God directing both the preaching of the gospel and the response to it?

📖 **Read Acts 16:16-24**

DICTIONARY

Divination (v 16): fortune-telling.

Salvation (v 17): being saved.

Advocate (v 21): recommend.

3. What do you think most disturbs the slave girl's owners?

Read Acts 16:25-40

DICTIONARY

Bonds (v 26): chains.
Magistrates (v 35): local legal officials.

Uncondemned (v 37): not proven to be guilty of anything.
Roman citizens (v 37): those with the right to a trial.

4. Trace through what happens in verses 25-34 and what the jailer is thinking and feeling.

Getting Personal | OPTIONAL

The jailer completely changes, not only in how he feels but in how he treats the other believers. When you became a Christian, did you see a similar change? How do you act toward other Christians now?

Paul and Silas leave in Philippi an unlikely band of disciples. A rich businesswoman, a slave girl, and a Gentile jailer make up the identity of the church. The power of God has brought people from all walks of life together into one faith.

Apply

5. Sometimes we feel that we just don’t know how to share the gospel with a particular person or in a particular setting. What help can we derive from the way God works in the lives of Lydia, the slave girl, and the jailer?

Investigate

📖 **Read Acts 17:1-15**

DICTIONARY

Custom (v 2): habit.
The Christ (v 3): the Messiah-figure long awaited by Jews.
Decrees (v 7): laws.
Conducted (v 15): went with, guided.

6. What is it that offends and upsets the Jews in Thessalonica?

7. How have Paul and Silas "turned the world upside down" in Macedonia? What do you think is the most subversive thing they have done or said?

📖 **Read Acts 17:16-21**

DICTIONARY

Provoked (v 16): angry.
Idols (v 16): statues of false gods.
Epicurean and Stoic (v 18): followers of two particular philosophies.
Divinities (v 18): gods.
Areopagus (v 19): rocky hill in Athens where trials and civic meetings took place.

8. How do we see that Paul's message is "strange" and "new" in Athens?

Read Acts 17:22-34

DICTIONARY

Inscription (v 23): words carved into stone.
Determined (v 26): decided, planned.
Repent (v 30): turn away from sin.
Assurance (v 31): certainty.

9. In what ways does Paul remain faithful to the truth and refuse to capitulate to Athenian ideas?

10. In what ways does Paul engage with Athenian culture in his speech, and why does he do so?

Explore More | OPTIONAL

Talk of Greek philosophies may seem to bear little significance for the church today, but they still exist in different forms and can even infect the Christian faith.

Epicureans thought that the gods didn't intervene in the world. Life was a matter of chance, and it was important to find pleasure where you could. Stoics, meanwhile, said that the world was controlled by fate: you weren't ultimately responsible for your own actions, and you had to just accept suffering. Both philosophies said that the soul alone, and not the body, was what counted, denying the dignity of the physical creation.

- How do these ideas contrast with Paul's message in verses 22-31?
- Can you see any of them creeping into the beliefs of Christians you know?

Getting Personal | OPTIONAL

Think of someone you know whose views or behavior are opposed to the gospel.

What is there in their life that does point to the truth? How could you use that to speak to them about Jesus?

Apply

11. What groups are there in your area with distinct social, religious, or ethnic backgrounds? Are there friendships across such divides in your church?

    - How could you equip yourselves to reach out to people in these groups faithfully and engagingly?

Pray

Use your answers to question 11 to help yourselves pray for people you know of different backgrounds.

4

God's Word Prevails

Acts 18:1 - 19:20

The Story So Far...

Sent by God, Paul took the gospel into the Gentile world. Some believed and others were hostile, but the missionaries returned rejoicing at all God had done.

False teachers threatened the true gospel by rejecting Gentile converts, but a council sought to unite believers around the truth.

Paul's mission in Macedonia turned the world upside down as many came to faith. In Greece Paul packaged his message to help the Athenians understand it.

Talkabout

1. What kinds of things do people have really strong views about? What drives them to try to make others see their point of view?

Investigate

Read Acts 18:1-17

DICTIONARY

Pontus (v 2): region in modern-day Turkey.
Claudius (v 2): emperor of Rome.
Achaia (v 12): region of southern Greece.
Tribunal (v 12): court of law.

2. In verses 9-10, how does God encourage Paul to go on speaking about what he is convinced of?

3. Looking both backwards and forwards in the chapter, why do you think Paul needs this encouragement?

Explore More | OPTIONAL

In verse 6 Paul refers to a description of a watchman's duties in Ezekiel.

Read Ezekiel 33:1-5

- How is Paul like the watchman described in this passage?

Paul says that he will go to the Gentiles rather than the Jews. Notice that this does not mean that no more Jews will hear the gospel. Two verses later, Crispus, a Jewish official, is converted through Paul's preaching.

Paul now leaves Corinth and travels back toward Antioch. Priscilla and Aquila accompany him part of the way, and while Paul travels on to Antioch, the main narrative stays in Ephesus with them.

Read Acts 18:18-28

DICTIONARY

Cenchreae (v 18): city near Corinth.
Vow (v 18): promise to God.
Eloquent (v 24): a good speaker.
Fervent (v 25): enthusiastic.
Grace (v 27): the gift of God.
Refuted (v 28): proved wrong.
Scriptures (v 28): the Old Testament.

4. Why do Priscilla and Aquila correct Apollos?

- What is the result?

5. Put yourself in the shoes of Priscilla and Aquila, or Apollos. How would you have felt?

- Why do you think they act as they do?

Getting Personal | OPTIONAL

Can you think of a time when someone has corrected your understanding of God? Did they do it well? What impact did it have?

6. Compare the encouragement given to Paul (v 9-10) with the correction given to Apollos (v 25-26). In each case, what threatens to hold back the word of God, and why does the truth win out?

Apply

7. In what settings are you most likely to be held back from speaking and acting in accordance with the truth? How can we make sure God's word wins?

Investigate

Read Acts 19:1-20

DICTIONARY

Speaking in tongues and prophesying (v 6): signs of the presence of the Holy Spirit.
Invoke (v 13): use a name.
Adjure (v 13): urge.
Extolled (v 17): lifted up, praised.
Divulging (v 18): revealing.
Prevail (v 20): succeed.

8. Luke describes the group Paul speaks to in Ephesus as "disciples." But what is lacking, and how serious is that lack?

The exorcists in verses 13-16 do not really know the one by whom Paul has power, so they try to invoke Jesus by appealing to Paul. They are attempting to leverage the name of Christ for their own ends—making money by casting out demons—without humbly submitting to the saving power of the gospel. The evil spirit recognizes that they are impostors.

9. Why do you think Luke tells us the value of the books burned in verse 19?

- How does this event help us to understand what repentance is?

10. Compare verses 1-7, 8-10, and 11-20. Very different things happen in each of these passages. But what is consistent about Paul's behavior?

11. Of all the signs we have seen of the strength of the word of the Lord and the name of Jesus in Ephesus, which do you think is the clearest?

Apply

12. Look back across chapter 19. Why is it a problem when as Christians we forget to think and talk about…
    - Jesus' power and his promise of blessing?

    - the cost and pain of repentance and discipleship?

- Which do you think your church is more likely to under- or over-emphasize?

Getting Personal | OPTIONAL

What can you do this week to encourage another believer to trust more in God's power, or to remember their need for repentance?

Pray

Pray for your church, your family, and your workplace.

Ask that the words of Acts 19:20 might prove as true where you live as they did in Ephesus.

Ask God to help you think of ways to uphold the truth in these different settings.

5

The God Worth Serving

Acts 19:21 - 20:38

The Story So Far...

Paul's first journey into the Mediterranean led to many coming to faith. The Jerusalem Council sought to unite Jewish and Gentile believers around the truth.

Paul's mission in Macedonia turned the world upside down as many came to faith. In Greece Paul packaged his message to help the Athenians understand it.

In Corinth Paul worked with Priscilla and Aquila, who later helped Apollos teach the truth, and corrected disciples in Ephesus, displaying the power of God's word.

Talkabout

1. What kinds of things are people proud of? How do they show their pride?

Investigate

Read Acts 19:21-41

DICTIONARY

Resolved (v 21): decided.
Disrepute (v 27): disgrace.
Deposed (v 27): brought down.
Asiarchs (v 31): ruling officials in the region of Asia.
Sacrilegious (v 37): breaking temple rules.
Blasphemers (v 37): those who speak badly of a god.

No city was as proud of its glorious structures as Ephesus was of its Temple of Artemis. It was one of the Seven Wonders of the Ancient World as it was the biggest building in existence: 130 x 67 meters (425 x 220 feet), supported by 127 marble columns.

2. Why is Demetrius worried about what Paul is saying (v 24-27)?

DICTIONARY

Asiarchs (v 31): ruling officials in the region of Asia.
Sacrilegious (v 37): breaking temple rules.
Blasphemers (v 37): those who speak badly of a god.

3. Compare the reaction of the crowds (v 28-34) to that of the town clerk (v 35-41). What is their attitude toward Artemis?

- Why do they respond differently to the Christian message?

4. What is Paul's priority in all of this?

5. Demetrius, the crowds, and the town clerk all say that Artemis is great. But what else do you think lies behind their actions? What desires fuel their worship of the goddess?

    - How does that compare with what drives Paul?

Apply

6. Think about the people you know and how their words and actions show what they really desire and worship. What do they daydream about, get excited about, prioritize, or fear?

Getting Personal | OPTIONAL

Think of some specific non-Christian friends. What do they worship? How could you talk to them about that?

Sometimes people are very confident about their worldview—whether their claim is that religion and science are incompatible, that the Scriptures are untrustworthy, or that believing in only one God is arrogant. But we should not let intimidation grip our hearts. Behind the confident tone may be nothing more than a foundation built on sand—as with the confused crowds in Ephesus. Good questions will reveal the shakiness of a person's worldview.

Investigate

📖 **Read Acts 20:1-16**

DICTIONARY

Assos, Miletus (v 13-15): cities of western Turkey.
Mytilene (v 14): city in Lesbos, an island.
Chios, Samos (v 15): islands near Turkey.
Pentecost (v 16): Jewish festival.

7. What do you think the believers think of the power Paul shows?

- Does it seem more or less important than his teaching?

8. In verses 1-6 and 13-16 we are given lots of details about Paul's journeys. Look back at 19:21. What shapes Paul's plans?

📖 **Read Acts 20:17-38**

DICTIONARY

Profitable (v 20): beneficial.
Afflictions (v 23): suffering.
Counsel (v 27): plan.
Admonish (v 31): warn, advise.
Sanctified (v 32): made holy.
Coveted (v 33): envied, desired.

Paul doesn't have time to return to Ephesus, but he wants to ensure that the church there has spiritually healthy elders. He draws the elders to himself and begins a commission which places the care of the congregation into their hands.

9. In verses 18-27, how does Paul describe the character of his work in Ephesus?

- In verses 33-35, how else does he say he has acted, and why?

Explore More | OPTIONAL

In his first letter to the Corinthians, Paul talks more about the way he lived among the churches he served.

Read 1 Corinthians 9:3-18

- What does Paul say he has a right to?
- Why does he give up those rights?

10. In Acts 20:28-32, how does Paul urge the Ephesian elders to lead the church well?

Getting Personal | OPTIONAL

What challenges you most in what Paul says here?

Choose one verse to remember that will help you to live in a way more worthy of God.

11. What does Paul's plan to go to Jerusalem tell us about his attitude toward his life?

Apply

12. How can we use our lives to display the fact that God alone is worthy of worship…
    - in what we say?
    - in how we plan?
    - in how we treat others?

Pray

Spend time worshiping God. To inspire your prayers, share with one another what it is that, for you, most makes it clear that the Lord Jesus is great.

Then use your answers to questions 6 and 12 to pray for the people you know and your own witness to them.

6

Accused in Jerusalem

Acts 21:1 - 23:35

The Story So Far...

Paul's first journey into the Mediterranean led to many coming to faith. The Jerusalem Council sought to unite Jewish and Gentile believers around the truth.

On his second and third journeys, Paul's consistent message transformed those who received it—both new converts and confused believers.

After a riot in Ephesus, Paul traveled on; he encouraged the churches, raised a dead man to life, and commissioned the Ephesian church leaders.

Talkabout

1. Can you think of specific times of difficulty in your life when God has helped you to be faithful to him and has worked through you to impact others?

Investigate

📖 **Read Acts 21:1-16**

NOTE: To save time, you could instead read the summary below the dictionary box, and then read aloud verses 12-16.

DICTIONARY

Cos, Rhodes (v 1): islands.
Patara (v 1): city in modern-day Turkey.
Tyre (v 3): city in modern-day Lebanon.
Ptolemais, Caesarea (v 7-8): cities in Judea.
The seven (v 8): leaders of the church in practical matters, chosen in Acts 6.
Bound (v 11): tied up.

The Spirit reveals to the Tyrian believers Paul's future destiny of arrest and suffering (v 4), just as he had to Paul (20:23). They try to persuade Paul to avoid the Spirit's leading to Jerusalem. In Caesarea the same thing happens again (21:10-12).

2. How does Paul feel about committing himself to his decision to go (v 13)?

📖 **Read Acts 21:17-26**

DICTIONARY

Zealous (v 20): passionate.
Forsake (v 21): abandon, betray.
Purify (v 24): here, undergo a religious rite.

3. Why are the elders of the Jewish church worried about what people think of Paul?

- What solution do they suggest to him?

Read Acts 21:27 – 22:22

NOTE: To save time, you could each read this long passage silently.

DICTIONARY

Defiled (21:28): dirtied.
Tribune of the cohort (v 31): high-ranking military official.
Centurion (v 32): middle-ranking military official.
Persecuted (22:4): attacked.

4. What is Paul accused of (21:28-29, 38)?

5. Acts 22:22 tells us that, until that point, the crowd listened to Paul. If you were a Jewish member of the crowd, what might you be thinking…
    - by the end of verse 5?
    - by the end of verse 16?
    - by the end of verse 21?

Getting Personal | OPTIONAL

Are there any areas right now in which you are under pressure—suffering or afraid or facing hostility? How could you continue steadfast in obedience? How could you use such circumstances to proclaim the gospel?

Apply

6. In what ways might the gospel message be offensive in our culture?

7. How can you make sure you remain faithful and put God first as you interact with others?

Investigate

📖 **Read Acts 22:23 – 23:11**

DICTIONARY

Flogging (22:24): whipping.
Contrary to (23:3): against.
Dissension (v 7): disagreement.

8. How does Paul take advantage of his background for the sake of the gospel...
    - in 22:25-30?

- in 23:6-10?

Getting Personal | OPTIONAL

Think about your background and your life so far. How has God worked in your life and your circumstances? How could you turn your experiences to a missionary purpose?

9. In 23:1-5, why does Paul speak angrily to the high priest?

- Why does he apologize?

Read Acts 23:12-35

NOTE: Again, you could each read this long passage silently to save time.

DICTIONARY

Oath (v 12): solemn promise.
Ambush (v 16): trap.
Governor (v 24): Roman ruler of entire region.
Disclosed (v 30): revealed.
Praetorium (v 35): headquarters.

10. Why does the tribune say that he is sending Paul to the Roman governor (v 26-30)?

11. Look back at verse 11. God speaks directly to Paul to outline his plans for him: to testify about him in Jerusalem and in Rome. Across all the passages in this study, what different things have contributed to the fulfillment of these plans?

Apply

12. How do we expect God to use us? Can you think of ways in which God could use...
    - your present circumstances (even if they seem bad)?
    - your faithful obedience in those circumstances?

Pray

Confess your areas of weakness and inability when it comes to remaining faithful and obedient.

Plead to God for courage and strength, asking him to give you confidence in and clarity about his will.

Reflecting on whatever circumstances you are currently in, pray that God will use them to his glory.

7

Hope on Trial

Acts 24:1 - 26:32

The Story So Far...

Paul was sent by God to preach Christ to Gentiles. His consistent message of repentance and belief caused both joy and uproar wherever he went.

After a riot in Ephesus, Paul traveled on; he encouraged the churches, raised a dead man to life, and commissioned the Ephesian church leaders.

Knowing the danger, Paul traveled to Jerusalem, where he was arrested after facing a mob. He used the opportunity to speak faithfully about God.

Talkabout

1. How would you sum up the gospel in three words?

Investigate

Read Acts 24:1-21

DICTIONARY

Detain (v 4): delay.
Sect (v 5): dangerous religious group.
Profane (v 6): treat disrespectfully.
Disputing (v 12): arguing.
Alms (v 17): gifts of money.
Tumult (v 18): uproar.

The case is made against Paul. His defense speech asserts his innocence and declares his hope in the resurrection of the dead.

2. What tactics does Tertullus use to try to persuade Felix?

3. How does Paul dismantle each of Tertullus' accusations?

4. Why is it important that Paul's conscience is clean (v 15-16)?

Explore More | OPTIONAL

Read 1 Peter 3:14-17

- Where in Acts 24 can you see Paul acting according to this advice?
  - "Have no fear of them, nor be troubled"
  - "In your hearts honor Christ the Lord as holy"
  - "Always being prepared to make a defense to anyone who asks you for a reason for the hope that is in you"
  - "Do it with gentleness and respect"
  - "Having a good conscience"

Read Acts 24:22 – 25:12

NOTE: To save time, you could each read this long passage silently.

DICTIONARY

Elapsed (24:27): passed.

Province (25:1): Roman administrative region.

5. Look at how Felix and then Festus respond to Paul. What are their reasons for treating him as they do?

God had revealed to Paul where he would send him to testify (23:11). He was to stand before governors, kings, and the emperor himself and proclaim the excellency of Christ. Paul's defense of himself and his appeal to Caesar are not intended to save his own neck but to promote the gospel.

Getting Personal | OPTIONAL

Have people ever made accusations against you because of your faith? How could you respond to such accusations in a way that points to the gospel, rather than simply to save your own skin?

Read Acts 25:13-27

DICTIONARY

Condemnation (v 15): guilty verdict.
Pomp (v 23): splendor, display.
Petitioned (v 24): made a request.

6. Why is Festus at a loss about Paul?

Apply

The Jews view Jesus as a great scandal which disrupts their entire religious culture. For the Romans, however, the tale of Jesus only leads to confusion.

7. How do people nowadays respond to the message of Jesus' resurrection from the dead, and why?

    - How can we prepare ourselves for these responses?

Investigate

📖 **Read Acts 26:1-23**

DICTIONARY

Controversies (v 3): disagreements, debates.
Attain (v 7): reach, gain.
Goads (v 14): sticks used to drive animals.
Delivering (v 17): rescuing.
Satan (v 18): the devil.

8. How does Paul explain the truth of the gospel?

9. How does Paul show the transformative power of the gospel in his own life?

10. How does Paul's own story exemplify the evangelistic message he presents in verses 18 and 23?

Getting Personal | OPTIONAL

How have you seen Christ work to transform you? How could you use your story as a tool for sharing the gospel?

Read Acts 26:24-32

The hearing began with Paul on trial. Now, however, his audience is under interrogation, as Paul confronts them with a summons to repent and believe in the gospel. He uses his innocence, not to gain release but to gain new opportunities to proclaim the resurrection of Christ.

11. Why does Paul think he is in a better situation than his audience (v 29)?

- Do Festus, Agrippa, and Bernice understand that?

Apply

12. In what ways and situations could you proclaim the hope that you have?

- How could the way you live bear witness to this hope?

Pray

Praise Jesus for his resurrection from the dead and all that that accomplished.

Ask God to continue to transform you and lead you into a godly way of living.

Pray for non-believing friends and family members, that God would draw them, like Paul, into repentance and bring them into his family.

Pray that God might use you to witness about Jesus to them.

8

Calm in the Storm

Acts 27:1 - 28:31

The Story So Far...

Paul was sent by God to preach Christ to Gentiles. His consistent message of repentance and belief caused both joy and uproar wherever he went.

Despite rioting and plots, Paul continued to encourage the churches and proclaim the truth. Arrested in Jerusalem, he spoke faithfully about God.

On trial before powerful men, Paul bore witness to the truth of Jesus' resurrection. After he appealed to Caesar, Festus agreed to send him to Rome.

Talkabout

1. What are some different ways in which people respond to difficulties?

Investigate

📖 **Read Acts 27:1-20**

DICTIONARY

Augustan Cohort (v 1): special unit of Roman army.
Sidon (v 3): city in modern-day Lebanon.
Lee (v 4): sheltered side.
Cnidus (v 7): coastal city in modern-day Turkey.
The Fast (v 9): Jewish festival.
Tempestuous (v 14): stormy.
Jettison (v 18): throw overboard.
Ship's tackle (v 19): equipment for sailing.
Tempest (v 20): storm.

The best seasons for navigating the Mediterranean are the spring and summer. But this trip took place during the fall, which presented a grave threat to the safety of the travellers. The danger rises and rises as we read.

2. What is the centurion's view of Paul on this part of the journey?

3. Look at what happens in verses 14-15, and how the sailors respond. How do the travelers feel by the end of verse 20?

📖 **Read Acts 27:21-44**

DICTIONARY

Incurred (v 21): experienced.
Fathom (v 28): about six feet or two meters.
Stern (v 28): back of a ship.
Perish (v 34): die.
Bow (v 30): front of a ship.
Rudders (v 40): steering equipment below the waterline.

4. How does Paul seem to feel, and why?

- How does this affect the way he behaves?

5. Trace the actions of the sailors and soldiers through the passage. How do you think their view of Paul—and his God—changes?

Apply

Paul's calmness stems from God's specific revelation (v 23-25). We don't have such specific promises, but we do have many others in the Bible which show us what God is providentially doing in all circumstances.

Look up Matthew 6:25-34; John 14:1-6; Romans 8:28-30; and Revelation 21:1-4.

6. How could these passages help us to share Paul's calm trust in the providence of God?

- What impact could this have on those around us?

Getting Personal | OPTIONAL

Reflect on your life and think of situations and circumstances in which you clearly saw or now recognize the Lord's providence. How does the reality of God's providence change the way you handle particular circumstances in your life?

Investigate

Read Acts 28:1-10

DICTIONARY

Dysentery (v 8): infection in the intestines.

7. What does the snakebite incident show us...
   - about Paul?
   - about God?

The Maltese people get confused between the two and conclude that Paul is actually a god. Luke does not provide much information about this or the other miracles at Malta. We can, however, deduce how God used these events. Paul could not perform any miracles without the power of God working in and through him. He would have stewarded the situation toward the gospel, as he did elsewhere (e.g. in Acts 14:8-18).

📖 Read Acts 28:11-16

DICTIONARY

Figurehead (v 11): wooden statue at the front of a ship.
Syracuse (v 12): city in Sicily.
Rhegium, Puteoli (v 12): cities in Italy.
Forum of Appius (v 15): a place 40 miles from Rome.
Compelled (v 19): forced.
Expounded (v 23): explained, preached.
Hindrance (v 31): obstacle.

8. What encourages Paul on this part of the journey?

📖 Read Acts 28:17-31

When Paul arrives in Rome, we might expect him to find a good attorney. After all, he has been brought there to be tried for his life. Instead, he calls local Jewish leaders together and speaks to them about hope.

9. In verses 17-20, how does Paul explain his circumstances to the Jewish leaders?

10. Why do the Jewish leaders respond in the way they do in verses 21-25?

- Do you think Paul is disappointed by their response?

11. Why do you think Luke ends the book so abruptly? What will happen next?

Getting Personal | OPTIONAL

God summons all his people to join him in the mission of salvation and be used by him as his ambassadors. We can trust God's sovereign will to advance the gospel. How will you answer his call this week?

Apply

12. How would you sum up the message of Acts 13 – 28 in a sentence?

- What has the Holy Spirit been challenging or encouraging you about in your own life as a result of reading this part of God's word?

Pray

Use your answers to question 12 to pray for one another.

Ask God to grant you the strength and courage to stand in the long line of Spirit-empowered, faithful witnesses which stretches all the way back to that unlikely band of 1st-century heroes.

Acts 13–28

The Church Multiplies

LEADER'S GUIDE

Leader's Guide: Introduction

This Leader's Guide includes guidance for every question. It will provide background information and help you if you get stuck. For each session, you'll also find the following:

The Big Idea: The main point of the session, in brief. This is what you should be aiming to have fixed in people's minds by the end of the session!

Summary: An overview of the passage you're reading together.

Optional Extra: Usually this is an introductory activity that ties in with the main theme of the Bible study and is designed to break the ice at the beginning of a session. Or it may be a "homework project" that people can tackle during the week.

Occasionally the Leader's Guide includes an extra follow-up question, printed in ***italics***. This doesn't appear in the main study guide but could be a useful add-on to help your group get to the answer or go deeper.

Here are a few key principles to bear in mind as you prepare to lead:

- Don't just read out the answers from the Leader's Guide. Ideally, you want the group to discover these answers from the Bible for themselves.
- Keep drawing people back to the passage you're studying. People may come up with answers based on their experiences or on teaching they've heard in the past, but the point of this study is to listen to God's word itself—so keep directing your group to look at the text.
- Make sure everyone finishes the session knowing how the passage is relevant for them. We do Bible study so that our lives can be changed by what we hear from God's word. So, **Apply** questions aren't just an add-on—they're a vital part of the session.

Finally, remember that your group is unique! You should feel free to use this Good Book Guide in a way that works for them. If they're a quiet bunch, you might want to spend longer on the **Talkabout** question. If they love to get creative, try using mind-mapping or doodling to kick-start some of your discussions. If your time is limited, you can choose to skip **Explore More** or split the whole session into two. Adapt the material in whatever way you think will help your group get the most out of God's word.

1

Mission Commenced

Acts 13:1 - 14:28

The Big Idea

As the Spirit inspires mission, we should welcome strong responses, whether positive or negative, as a sign of God's work.

Summary

In Paul's first missionary journey, the gospel begins its advance throughout the Mediterranean world. It all starts at a gathering of the believers in Antioch (13:1-3), where we see the Holy Spirit commission Paul and Barnabas to preach.

Luke compresses the history in places to keep the narrative moving, but also homes in on certain specific events. First, at Paphos in Cyprus, a Roman official comes to faith despite the opposition of a magician (v 6-12). Such anti-missionary efforts will span the rest of the narrative, but they never deter Paul and Barnabas from proclaiming the good news.

Next they make it to Pisidian Antioch, a city in the region of Galatia, and Paul preaches in the synagogue (v 13-43). His concluding words reveal the incredible significance of responses to the preached word. There is no neutral response: anything less than repentance amounts to a rejection of God. As he expected, many Jews respond with revulsion, while non-Jews joyfully accept the good news (v 44-48). Luke records a watershed moment in the Acts narrative as Paul announces that the gospel will advance to the Gentile world, establishing the validity of his mission in the prophetic witness of Isaiah (v 47).

As the journey continues into chapter 14, the pattern of Paul's preaching strategy meets a similar pattern of belief contrasted with opposition. In Lystra the responses are still more extreme. After Paul heals a cripple, the crowds want to worship him and Barnabas as gods (v 8-18); yet verse 19 shatters the scene as Paul goes from denying his identity as a god to being dragged out of the city and almost stoned to death.

The missionaries end their journey by retracing their steps to encourage and strengthen the new believers (v 21-25). As they finally come home to Antioch, they encourage their sending church and tell them of the glorious testimony of God's saving power (v 26-28). The opposition they have encountered and the suffering they have endured only serve to confirm their confidence in the Lord.

As we read of this first mission to the Gentiles, we too can rejoice and gain confidence. The message that Paul shared is the same one that has come to us; the Spirit who sent and accompanied him is the same one who dwells in us. We too should have a zeal for gospel proclamation, and we too should count it an honor to suffer for the gospel.

Optional Extra

Ask the group to share examples of people who inspire them because of their perseverance in the face of opposition. Here are some Christian examples to look up to get you started: Elisabeth Elliot; William Tyndale; Brother Andrew; Gladys Aylward.

Guidance for Questions

1. **Think of a time when you have had good news to share. What responses did people have?**
   This question aims first to capture the excitement of sharing good news and then to prepare the group for discussions later about negative responses to the gospel and how we should respond to them.

- **How would it have felt if they simply hadn't believed you?**
  Some people might have been upset. Others might have sought to convince them. Others would simply have gone off to tell someone else instead. Would anyone be so demoralized that they wouldn't tell anyone else?

2. **What starts Saul and Barnabas off on their missionary journey?**
   It all begins when the people of God in Antioch seek his name through fasting and prayer. God answers, and the Holy Spirit speaks of his will for the consecration of Barnabas and Saul for a mission of gospel proclamation. This starts the mass movement of the gospel which will be described in the second half of Acts.

3. **What is the missionaries' strategy to begin with (v 5-6)?**
   Luke tells us that they begin by preaching in the synagogues, where they share a common religious background with their hearers. This strategy of preaching first to the Jews demonstrates their careful and reasoned approach. They make their way to Paphos, which was the seat of power in Cyprus.

4. **Trace the responses of the proconsul and the magician through the passage.**
   The proconsul is initially interested, but the magician tries to influence him away from the message of the gospel. But no amount of hostility will hinder the missionaries' zeal for gospel proclamation. Through a display of God's power and through the preached word, the proconsul eventually repents and believes in Jesus as his Savior.

5. **Consider how we see God working and how he uses people in this first part of Paul and Barnabas' mission. In what ways might this affect how we think about and do evangelism ourselves?**
   - The mission arises out of a prayer meeting as the disciples worship God together. *Do we give enough time to worshiping and praying together? Do we have high enough expectations of our fellowship and how God can use it?*
   - The missionaries are sent out with the disciples' prayers (v 3) and by

the Holy Spirit (v 4). *Do we pray for one another as we go into the world? Do we remember that God goes with us for mission?*

- As discussed in question 3, the missionaries have a strategy. *Do we share this careful approach?*
- Paul and Barnabas go to Cyprus, which is where Barnabas comes from (Acts 4:36). *Do we think of our homes and familiar places as mission fields?*
- They enlist a helper. This is John Mark, who will later write the Gospel of Mark. God can powerfully use relationships like these towards his kingdom. *Do we welcome people into our mission and seek to train and support one another?*
- Paul, filled with the Spirit, is passionate about the truth of the gospel (v 10). *Do we share this zeal and clarity? Could we pray for it more?*
- God uses the opposition of the magician to bring the proconsul to faith. *Are we demoralized by opposition or do we ask God to use it?*

6. What is Paul's concluding message (v 38-41)? How do you think you would have felt to hear it?

Paul emphasizes the opportunity to be forgiven and the importance of a response. Salvation comes by faith in the only one who fulfilled the Jewish law's demands perfectly. Paul preaches the chain-breaking power of Christ's ministry, which secures freedom for all who believe in him. His concluding words show us that there is no such thing as a neutral response to the gospel. It demands repentance and faith; anything less amounts to a rejection of God's grace.

Explore More

- ***Look more carefully at the rest of Paul's sermon. Can you map out his argument? Try dividing it as follows: verses 16-22; verses 23-25; verses 26-27; verses 28-37.***
  - *v 16-22: Paul takes his audience back through the story of the Old Testament.*
  - *v 23-25: He reminds them of John the Baptist and claims that God's promises are fulfilled in Jesus.*
  - *v 26-27: He roots the identity of Jesus, and his rejection in Jerusalem, in the Scriptures.*
  - *v 28-37: He recounts the death, burial, and resurrection of Jesus, showing how God's word points to his ministry.*

7. After the gospel is preached, who feels joy, and why?

Jesus' disciples are filled with joy as the gospel is accepted and the Holy Spirit is received (v 52). The people of Pisidian Antioch initially respond with interest, but after the Jews speak out in rejection of the message, it is only the Gentiles who receive it and are filled with joy (v 48). The new disciples, along with the missionaries, continue to experience joy even after they meet persecution because the gospel has still been proclaimed and God's purposes fulfilled.

8. **What patterns do you notice in the way the gospel is preached and received? Try comparing these verses with 13:1-12, 48-52.**
   Paul and Barnabas continue their strategy of starting at the synagogue. Their bold preaching is authenticated by physical displays of God's power. They are met with both belief and hostility, the latter especially from the Jews. Despite this persecution, they have a single-minded vision; nothing will stop them.

9. **What is different about what happens in Lystra, and what remains the same?**
   The crowds respond positively but inappropriately. Thinking that the miracle demonstrates something about Paul rather than something about God, they begin to worship Paul and Barnabas. The key thing that remains the same is the missionaries' faithful preaching: Paul seizes the opportunity to clarify the gospel. Again, there is a hostile and violent response; even eloquence and flawless wisdom cannot cure spiritual blindness.

10. **How would you sum up all that has happened to Paul and Barnabas so far in these two chapters?**
    It may help group members to take a moment to look back through what they have read in this session. Ask everyone to write down a one-sentence answer before sharing. You could encourage them to try answering the question from different perspectives: What have Paul and Barnabas done? What has God done? How have people responded?

11. **How do Paul and Barnabas themselves sum up their mission (v 27)?**
    Paul and Barnabas encourage their sending church and tell them of the glorious testimony of God's saving power. They have suffered; they could have returned defeated and broken, angry and frustrated that such calamity would befall faithful servants of Christ. Instead, they recognize the fact that God has used their suffering to win many new believers.

12. **How do these chapters encourage us to keep on sharing the truth about Jesus?**
    Like Paul, we can be certain that we are doing God's will as we speak faithfully about him. Like him, we have the Holy Spirit to sustain and support us. Whether people respond with belief, confusion, or hostility, we can remember the early disciples' joy and give thanks that God is glorified in our suffering as well as our success.

    - **How can we help each other to remember these encouragements?**
      Ask group members to share specific ways they'd like help to remember. Help them to make plans so that they do!

2

The Council in Jerusalem

Acts 15:1 - 16:5

The Big Idea

We must hold firmly to the truth that we are saved only by God's grace, not by our actions; the gospel is for all people of any background. Yet we must also act, in order to strengthen the church, in a way that subordinates our preferences to others' needs.

Summary

In Acts 15, false teachers claim that obedience to the Law of Moses is necessary for salvation (v 1-5). A council of church leaders convenes in Jerusalem to discuss and deal with this claim (v 6). They know that a tainted gospel is no gospel at all.

Peter addresses the meeting first to establish a sound theological answer to these false teachers and demonstrate the beauty of the gospel in tearing down dividing walls of ethnic identity (v 7-11). It is only by grace that anyone can be saved, Jew or Gentile.

After Paul and Barnabas recapitulate the spread of the gospel in the Gentile world (v 12), James stands up to conclude the council (v 13-21). He adds to Peter's words by grounding the salvation of the Gentiles in the Old Testament: God's plan of redemption was always to rebuild the house of David using people from all nations. The false teachers are clearly wrong. James also sets out moral instructions for the Gentiles to observe. Although following these instructions is not necessary for the Gentiles to be saved, it will help them not to provoke and offend Jewish Christians. All believers are called to subordinate personal preferences to the needs of others, as the power of the gospel builds a multinational and multiethnic church.

Ambassadors are chosen to deliver these instructions to the Gentile believers (v 22-30). Besides pastoral concern, their letter expresses confidence that it is the Spirit who has inspired their conclusions and is protecting the church. The Gentile Christians respond with joy; the distillation of the true gospel strengthens the faith and solidifies the unity of the Antioch disciples (v 31-35).

Paul now decides to visit the churches he has planted but disagrees with Barnabas about whether to bring John Mark along with them. This results in a separation (v 36-41). Despite this bitterness, neither gives up on the mission to which God has called them; both go to visit and strengthen the believers.

Acts 16 opens with an introduction to Paul's protégé, Timothy, who undergoes circumcision. This is not for his salvation but for the sake of the Jews to whom they will preach (v 1-3). Timothy demonstrates the heart of an evangelist and servant of Christ, willing to do whatever it takes to see people come to saving faith.

Optional Extra

It could help the group to begin to imagine what it feels like to be excluded by arbitrary rules, as the Gentiles are by the false teachers in our passage. So here is an icebreaker about imposing rules. Explain to the group that they must each come up with an item to buy at an imaginary shop. It must comply with your rule, but you will not tell them what the rule is. The rule is that the item must begin with the first letter of the person's name (so Rob could buy a radish or a radio, while Cathy could buy a carrot or a candle). Go round the group and tell each person whether their item complies with the rule. As people keep suggesting items, they will gradually work out what the rule is. Keep going until everyone has worked it out!

Guidance for Questions

1. **People have conflicts and disagreements about all kinds of things. Which are worth fighting over, and which aren't? Why do we find it hard to remember which is which?**
   You might discuss serious moral issues such as infidelity in marriage or an unfair dismissal at work; conflicts of opinion between team members or friends; and petty disagreements in the home. As we deal with conflict, we are caught between the desire to carry our point and the desire to maintain good relations with the other person. In the heat of the moment, it can be hard to evaluate our own motivations. When we press our point, is it just out of pride, or is there something more important at stake? When we back down, is it just out of cowardice, or are we thinking about how to serve and encourage the other person?

2. **What does Luke tell us about the people in verses 1 and 5?**
   These people are from Judea, which is perhaps why it is in Jerusalem, in Judea, that the ensuing discussions take place. They are Pharisees—the most conservative faction of the Jews at that time. But they are also believers. Given that the Pharisees are so hostile in the Gospels, the fact that some repented and believed in Christ should give us cause to rejoice! However, these believers mistakenly maintain their focus on the Law of Moses.

3. **What does Peter say about being cleansed (v 8-9)?**
   Peter points to the centrality of the heart. What makes us acceptable to God is not ceremonial purity but a cleansed heart: one cleansed by the blood of Jesus Christ. Anyone, whether or not they observe the Law of Moses, can be made clean by Jesus.

4. **What other reasons does he give for not imposing obedience to the Law of Moses on the Gentiles?**
   - v 7: Peter refers to the vision in which God revealed to him the inclusion of Gentiles in the promise, and to the conversion of Cornelius, a

Gentile, which sealed that promise. Ask the group to read Acts 10 to understand what Peter means.

- 15:8: Peter sees the evidence of the Holy Spirit in the Gentile believers, which serves as the authenticating seal of God's presence; they have already been saved, without circumcision.
- v 10: Peter exposes the hypocrisy of these Jews, who would dare to place the burden of the law on Gentiles when the Jews themselves had failed to keep its requirements.

Explore More

- ***Read Romans 3:20-25. What is it that brings righteousness?***
  The Law of Moses never brought righteousness but only made people aware of their sin (v 20-21). Regardless of who we are (v 23), we can gain righteousness only through Christ (v 22, 24), and be forgiven only because of faith in him (v 25).
- ***Read Romans 4:3, 9-12. Why is it incorrect to say that circumcision is necessary to be saved?***
  It did not save Abraham; only faith did (v 3). All subsequent believers, whether circumcised or uncircumcised, would also be made righteous only by faith (v 11-12).
- ***What then was the purpose of circumcision (v 11-12)?***
  For Abraham, circumcision was a sign of the righteousness he had already gained by faith in God. Paul is referring to God's original command in Genesis 17:9-11.

5. **In verses 15-18, what argument does James add?**
James grounds the salvation of the Gentiles not in Paul's testimony of their conversion, nor in Peter's vision, but in the Old Testament. The Gentile inclusion is a prophetic fulfillment long ago declared in the Hebrew Scriptures.

6. **What do you think is James' motivation here?**
James does not call into question the salvation of the Gentile believers but does seek to appease the Pharisee Christians. He is asking Gentiles to love their Jewish brothers and sisters by not intentionally provoking them.

7. **Is there anything in our churches that could give the wrong impression to non-Christians about the importance of the way we act?**
   - Christians can tend toward a Pharasaical view of the gospel, whereby obedience to God has eclipsed our view of and our need for the cross. Sometimes non-believers assume that Christians think we must be good people in order to be saved. Ask the group to think carefully about specific ways in which your church might be accidentally confirming that impression.
   - At the same time, we must not let our rest in the grace of God lead to a flippant life, but we should think

carefully about how to obey God and serve one another. Jesus paid a terrible price, which his people ignore or belittle when they view salvation as cheap and holiness as optional. The result is that the name of the Lord is dishonored (Romans 2:23-24).

8. **If you had been a Gentile believer in Antioch, how would you have been encouraged as you received the news from Jerusalem?**

   The letter from the Jerusalem Council is designed to build up the Gentile believers:
   - It makes it clear that the Pharisee Christians did not come on the authority of the leaders of the church (v 24).
   - It exudes compassion for the Gentile believers, taking note of the difficulty they have found themselves in (v 24).
   - It dignifies Paul and Barnabas, representatives of Antioch, as beloved brothers in faith (v 25-26).
   - It grounds the impetus of its claims in the authority of the Holy Spirit, who protects the church and its doctrine (v 28).
   - Rather than simply demanding conformity, the letter points to the flourishing that will result from following its recommendations (v 29).

9. **What motivates Paul? What do you think motivates Barnabas?**

   Paul wants to strengthen the churches. He knows the challenges of the road before him and, given what happened previously, he does not view Mark as suited for the task. He needs people with proven conviction, solidarity, and readiness to die for the gospel. Meanwhile, Barnabas exudes sympathy and forgiveness. This is consistent with the fact that he was also the first disciple in Jerusalem to accept Paul as a brother in Christ (Acts 9:26-27).

   - **Do you think they disagree well?**

     Paul and Barnabas seem to separate in bitterness, not on good terms. This is a tragedy. Separation in mission must be done in godliness and holiness. However, neither Paul nor Barnabas gives up on the mission or the task to which God has called them. They both go on to visit and strengthen the believers in Cyprus and in Syria and Cilicia (v 39-41).

   - ***OPTIONAL: What does 2 Timothy 4:11 tell us about Paul's attitude to Mark?***

     By the end of his life, Paul was reconciled with Mark. If we disagree, we should remain open to reconciliation as the result of change in either party.

10. **Why do you think Paul feels it is important to circumcise Timothy?**

    Just like James' decree encouraging Gentile believers to keep to certain purity laws, Timothy's circumcision is a way of avoiding offense to Jews. Timothy's mother was a Jew, and so she had violated the Old Testament law by failing to have him circumcised; Jews, knowing this, would question his identity and integrity as a Jew. Paul knows that for Timothy to have the kind of authority and respect that would be required of him in ministry—especially in ministry to the Jews—he must be circumcised.

Explore More

- ***Read 1 Corinthians 8:4-13. How does an attitude like Paul's help believers?***
  Paul knows that there is no problem with eating food that has been offered to an idol, because idols are not real. However, other Christians believe that it is wrong to eat such food. Paul acknowledges that to eat it could confuse these Christians and lead them to do something which they believe to be wrong. Therefore it is better to surrender the right to eat pagan temple food, for the sake of these Christians.

- ***Read 1 Corinthians 9:19-23. How does it advance the gospel?***
  By behaving like others (as Timothy does by being circumcised), Paul is more likely to gain an audience and win them for Christ.

11. What divides Christians today? How can we strengthen the church in the face of this? Think about how this applies to your church specifically.

- Your group could think about the style and practical methods of different churches; differences in understanding secondary issues in theology (such as the place of baptism) between branches of the church; or categories which divide society in general, such as ethnicity or age.
- We must stand up for the truth that salvation is through the grace of the Lord Jesus alone (15:11) and transcends barriers between people.
- We must never permit false teaching, in our own hearts or in our churches, but stand on the confidence of God's Spirit-inspired word.
- We must have compassion and submit ourselves to the needs of those around us; if an action causes offense, we should abstain from it, even if it is not sinful in itself (15:19; 1 Corinthians 8:8-13).
- We must accept that sometimes, like Paul and Barnabas, gospel laborers need to separate—either because of doctrinal difference or because of personal issues. We must not be surprised by this but must seek to do it in godliness and in holiness, honoring Christ.

3

The World Upside Down

Acts 16:6 - 17:34

The Big Idea

Since it is God who brings people to faith, we should confidently present the gospel to people of all backgrounds, being sensitive but not submissive to their worldviews.

Summary

As Paul, Silas, and Timothy continue their journeys, the Spirit directs them to Philippi in Macedonia (16:6-12). There they meet Lydia, a wealthy, religious Gentile. She hears Paul preaching the gospel and becomes a Christian (v 13-15). Luke tells us that it is God who "opened her heart"; Paul has the privilege of preaching to her, but it is God's work that he is doing.

After opening the hearts of Lydia and her household, the Lord then works in some very unlikely characters. First (v 16-18), a slave girl is delivered from a demon. Next (v 19-34), after Paul and Silas are thrown into prison for allegedly preaching illegally, their jailer comes to faith; he is amazed by their incredible response to imprisonment, as first they sing hymns of praise and then they refuse to leave after an earthquake shatters their chains.

Paul and Silas are released and visit the other new Christians in the city (v 35-40). These diverse believers are newly united in Christ.

Chapter 17 gives us further demonstrations of the versatility of the gospel as the one message of truth which can reach diverse people and different cultures. Verses 1-14 see the missionaries travel through other cities in Macedonia. Paul's presentation of the gospel has a powerful effect on crowds, leading to a riot in Thessalonica and the accusation that the apostles are turning the world upside down. Berea sees strong responses too. Paul then escapes to Athens (v 15).

In addition to visiting the synagogue, Paul also goes to the crowds in the marketplace in Athens (v 16-21). He interacts with philosophers there and is then brought to the Areopagus, or Mars Hill, to speak to them more fully. His speech shows that he does not have a rigid format and style of communication for the gospel (v 22-31). We can maintain the truth while packaging our message to meet the needs of a particular audience. As Paul explains to the Athenians, all humanity, even while lost in sin, still bears the image of God. All people can come to know him.

Optional Extra

Test your group's cultural awareness by asking them to guess the meaning of idioms from different languages. Read the idiom and ask everyone to write down what they think it means, while you write down the actual meaning. Shuffle together all the pieces of paper, read them all out, and hold a vote on the correct one.

- *To seize the moon by the teeth*—to try the impossible (French)
- *To hang noodles on someone's ears*—to fool someone (Russian)
- *To walk like a cat around hot porridge*—to talk without ever getting to your point (Swedish)
- *A dog in church*—an unwanted guest (Italian)

Guidance for Questions

1. **How diverse are the people you know? How do their backgrounds or values influence the way you relate to them?**
   We often naturally alter what we say as we talk to different people. Get the group to give specific examples of this—what changes when they talk to someone whose first language isn't English, for example? What about someone of very different political views or social background? What should stay the same as we talk to people of different backgrounds, and what should change?

2. **How do we see God directing both the preaching of the gospel and the response to it?**
   First, as the missionaries travel, the Holy Spirit directs them, first preventing them from going to certain parts of Asia (v 6) and Bithynia (v 7), and then leading them to Philippi in Macedonia (v 8-12). Second, when Lydia becomes a Christian, God is the one who opens her heart (v 14).

3. **What do you think most disturbs the slave girl's owners?**
   - They are angry about the miraculous healing of the slave girl; it spells financial disaster for them because her fortune-telling ability has come to an end (v 16, 19).
   - Perhaps they are also disturbed by the healing itself. Where they exploited their slave and were pleased by the presence of the evil spirit inside her, Paul releases her. Although her claims are true, he knows that his message flows from the authority of Christ, not of Satan. Unlike the slave owners, he will not exploit the presence of this spirit. The girl is delivered by the power of Jesus.
   - But the reason the slave owners give for their outrage is a legal one (v 20-21). Jews had been expelled from Rome by the Emperor Claudius, and promoting Judaism was illegal throughout the empire. Since Christianity at this point was seen as a subset of Judaism, Christian evangelism was breaking the law.

4. **Trace through what happens in verses 25-34 and what the jailer is thinking and feeling.**
   Depending on the size of the group, you could go round in a circle, asking each person to say what happens next.
   - v 25: Paul and Silas sing and pray.

- v 26: An earthquake opens the doors of the prison and breaks everyone's chains.
- v 27: The jailer assumes that his prisoners have all run away; he prepares to kill himself because death was the punishment for letting prisoners escape.
- v 28: But Paul cries out to him to stop.
- v 29: The jailer is still afraid but for a different reason. He has recognized the supernatural nature of the earthquake and the uniqueness of Paul and Silas as prisoners, as evidenced first by their praying and singing, and then by their staying in the cells. He knows that something inexplicable has occurred. He has seen the power of the Lord around him and in Paul and Silas. And so...
- v 30: He is ready to hear the word of God.
- v 31-34: He and his entire household hear the message of the gospel, believe, and are baptized. A sign of their transformation is the way they care for Paul and Silas and the joy they express.

5. **Sometimes we feel that we just don't know how to share the gospel with a particular person or in a particular setting. What help can we derive from the way God works in the lives of Lydia, the slave girl, and the jailer?**
   - In the story of Lydia, we see that Paul is the one who shares the message, but God is the one who brings salvation. God has chosen us, too, as his ambassadors, and we can join his mission with joy, knowing that his power is at work.
   - In the story of the slave girl, we see the power of God to deliver people from evil. It is easy to feel powerless in the face of an evil world, but we should persist in praying for non-Christians in the name of Jesus.
   - In the story of the jailer, we see how the characters of Paul and Silas provide a powerful testimony of God. Likewise, we should seek to live godly lives, in order to gain the opportunity to witness to Christ with our words too.

   You could pause to pray here about those people to whom, and settings in which, group members find it difficult to speak about Jesus.

6. **What is it that offends and upsets the Jews in Thessalonica?**
   - The Jews were expecting a Christ who would come as a national king and military leader. The idea which Paul presents, of the Messiah dying on a Roman cross instead of conquering Rome, may be what offends the Jewish worldview (v 2-3).
   - They are not only offended because of Paul's message but also because of the powerful effect it has on the crowd (v 4-5). They don't want people to stop listening to them in order to listen to Paul instead.
   - Finally, like the slave owners in chapter 16, they accuse the Christians of acting illegally (v 6-7).

7. **How have Paul and Silas "turned the world upside down" in Macedonia? What do you think is the most subversive thing they have done or said?**

   You could ask group members to go through all you have read so far in this session on their own or in pairs, highlighting verses which show Paul and Silas turning the world upside down; then discuss together. Look out for the following:

   - individual lives being transformed
   - Paul and Silas behaving counter-culturally
   - their message subverting or challenging what people think
   - whole cities being affected

8. **How do we see that Paul's message is "strange" and "new" in Athens?**

   First, in Paul's strong reaction to Athenian culture. He sees the false worship all over the city and is provoked and disgusted by it. His own behavior and beliefs are very different from the norms here. Second, in the response of the philosophers. Some seem confused and some dismissive (v 18). Others treat Paul's message as a curiosity (v 19-21). None of them are at all familiar with what he is saying.

9. **In what ways does Paul remain faithful to the truth and refuse to capitulate to Athenian ideas?**

   - Paul calls the Athenians' idols "objects of your worship" rather than "gods," because he knows they are no deities (v 23). In verse 29 he goes further, actively condemning the worship of man-made idols.
   - Paul asserts the Athenians' ignorance of the true God and starts explaining what God is really like (v 23-26). He proclaims that there is one God who is the "Lord of heaven and earth." He challenges the common view that gods are limited to temples and need to be worshiped there. He insists on the doctrine of creation (v 24-26).
   - He continues by pointing to the Athenians' sin and the need they have for repentance (v 30).
   - Finally, Paul does not omit the doctrine of the resurrection of the dead (v 31), although he knows they will not respond well to it.

10. **In what ways does Paul engage with Athenian culture in his speech, and why does he do so?**

    - He starts by engaging with the Athenians' own beliefs (v 22-23), finding an idea (the altar to an unknown god) from which he can build a bridge to the gospel message.
    - He does not mention the Messiah or quote from Scripture; these things might make sense to a Jewish audience but would be meaningless to the Athenian philosophers.
    - He asserts that it is possible for all people, including Athenians, to seek and find God (v 26-27).
    - He finds truth in the Athenians' culture, quoting from a pagan poet to illustrate his point (v 28).

Paul never compromises on the truth, but he presents it in such a way that the Athenians can comprehend it. He does not want anything to hinder the gospel from reaching the hearts and minds of his audience. The gospel itself should be the only possible stumbling block, not the way it is presented.

Explore More

- ***How do these ideas contrast with Paul's message in verses 22-31?***
  - *Paul describes an all-powerful God (v 24), which may seem similar to the Stoic idea of fate. But the truth is that humans are still responsible for their actions: we must still "seek God" (v 27) and obey him.*
  - *Paul affirms the glory of the created world, which helps us to seek God (v 26-27). We should acknowledge that creation is good and await the new creation, where we will have new physical bodies.*
- ***Can you see any of them creeping into the beliefs of Christians you know?***

  Some Christians seek a nirvana-style spirituality and try to ignore the physical world. But we are told to develop trust in God through active spiritual disciplines—Bible-reading, prayer, fellowship, and the fight against sin.

---

11. **What groups are there in your area with distinct social, religious, or ethnic backgrounds? Are there friendships across such divides in your church?**

    You could find out more about such groups in advance and share the information now to help yourselves to pray.

- **How could you equip yourselves to reach out to people in these groups faithfully and engagingly?**

  Like Paul, we should be clear on the truth of the gospel, which can turn the world upside down. At the same time, we can try to think of ways to engage directly with the worldviews of different people. How can we make sure that only the inherent challenge of the gospel message can be a stumbling block, and not the way we present it?

4

God's Word Prevails

Acts 18:1 - 19:20

The Big Idea

We must not be afraid to uphold the truth of God, correcting and teaching each other as well as speaking to non-believers.

Summary

Paul's journey shifts to Corinth (18:1-17) and then Ephesus (18:18 – 19:41). He stays for a long time in both places, with the result that "the word of the Lord continued to increase and prevail mightily" (19:20).

In Corinth he meets Priscilla and Aquila, a Jewish couple and believers in Christ. He moves in with them, works with them as a tentmaker, and preaches in the synagogue. Once again Paul faces rejection as well as acceptance, and in 18:9-10 the Lord appears to him and encourages him to press on. Paul must preach the truth and not be silent; he has been called to Corinth, and the Lord will keep him safe there.

So after the tumult of rejection dies down (v 12-17), Corinth continues to serve as Paul's residence for some time. But eventually he returns to Antioch, accompanied part of the way by Priscilla and Aquila (v 18-22).

Luke's narrative next takes a break from the ministry of Paul and shifts to Apollos, Priscilla, and Aquila in Ephesus (v 24-28). Apollos is a well-educated, eloquent believer, but something remains deficient about his instruction, and Priscilla and Aquila take him aside to correct him. His humble acceptance of this correction leads to the strengthening of many believers.

Paul now arrives in Ephesus and finds disciples with an understanding even more deficient than that of Apollos. Paul questions and teaches them, and they come to a saving faith (19:1-7).

Once again Paul meets with rejection in the synagogue, and goes instead to the hall of Tyrannus, a school of rhetoric, where he and his followers spend two years preaching the word of God and making new disciples (v 8-10). God accomplishes glorious things through the power of Paul's ministry, performing miracles through him (v 11-12). Some Jewish exorcists try to get in on the business and invoke the name of Jesus, but because they have not truly accepted Jesus, they are humiliated (v 13-16). The result of this extraordinary encounter with the power of God is remarkable: many believers who have been mixing magical arts with devotion to Christ are convicted of their idolatry by the Holy Spirit (v 17-20). They come confessing and bringing their paraphernalia of witchcraft and divination to be burned.

These scenes should lead us to greater devotion to the word of God—to speaking out about Jesus accurately and faithfully. This is what we have been called to do; the gospel spreads by faithful preaching. We must also encourage other Christians in Christ-likeness by promoting the truth of the gospel within the church: the power, and the cost, of following Jesus.

Optional Extra

Each person must present two truths and one lie about themselves. The rest must guess which is the lie. The point is that it is important to know the truth!

Guidance for Questions

1. **What kinds of things do people have really strong views about? What drives them to try to make others see their point of view?**
   People have strong views about politics, about lifestyle choices, about films or books or music, and about many other things. They may become convinced because of their own experiences or because of arguments they have heard from others; they may be driven predominantly by emotion or more by reasoned thought. Sometimes they share their opinions because they are angry that others hold a different point of view; sometimes it is because they want to help or look after others.

2. **In verses 9-10, how does God encourage Paul to go on speaking about what he is convinced of?**
   The Lord reminds Paul that he need not be afraid. He commands him to go on speaking. Paul can preach with confidence knowing that he is serving God; he would only fail if he remained silent. Paul must put his trust in God's power, provision, and sovereign will; the Lord is with him and will protect him, and will bring many to faith.

3. **Looking both backwards and forwards in the chapter, why do you think Paul needs this encouragement?**
   - In verse 6 the Jews oppose Paul, and he is forced to give up on preaching to them. Paul responds confidently, knowing that he is responsible only for ensuring people hear the word, and not for the way they respond to it. Yet it seems that Paul did need comfort after this rejection.
   - Later, the Jews in Corinth make the same accusation before the Roman rulers that others have made before (v 13; see 16:20-21; 17:6-7). Previously this resulted in violence. Paul needs to remember the promise of verse 10: that God is with him and no one will harm him. Sure enough, the proconsul dismisses the case. God works in the situation and protects Paul.

Explore More

- ***Read Ezekiel 33:1-5. How is Paul like the watchman described in this passage?***
  Paul has proclaimed the impending danger: spiritual separation from God. But the Jews have heard

the trumpet call of the gospel and chosen to reject it. Thus, Paul is doing exactly what he has been called to do; the people's rejection, resistance, and blasphemy are now their own responsibility.

---

4. **Why do Priscilla and Aquila correct Apollos?**
   Apollos was a gifted and well-educated speaker. However, his knowledge only extended to the teachings of John the Baptist. John's teaching was incomplete because it predicted and anticipated the ministry of the Messiah. So Apollos' preaching could have led many astray.

- **What is the result?**
  In verses 27-28 we see the fruit of Apollos' humble acceptance of the intervention. When Apollos arrives in Achaia, his preaching has an even greater effect and strengthens the church enormously. His own eloquence and education, combined with the accurate knowledge of the truth which Priscilla and Aquila have given him, serve to make him a powerful witness to the Jews and a strong support to the other believers.

5. **Put yourself in the shoes of Priscilla and Aquila, or Apollos. How would you have felt?**
   Priscilla and Aquila were strangers in Ephesus, and it must have been tempting to remain silent, fearing a harsh response from Apollos. Meanwhile, Apollos had been preaching his heart out about Jesus and probably didn't expect to be pulled aside and corrected. He could have responded with anger and resentment.

- **Why do you think they act as they do?**
  Priscilla and Aquila know what the truth is, and they put that first. Apollos accepts their instructions because he has profound maturity and humility. He too is devoted to God above himself.

6. **Compare the encouragement given to Paul (v 9-10) with the correction given to Apollos (v 25-26). In each case, what threatens to hold back the word of God, and why does the truth win out?**
   - Paul is held back by fear. Apollos is held back by lack of understanding.
   - God encourages Paul directly, giving him reasons to trust him. Paul hears this word and believes it. Apollos, meanwhile, is encouraged by his brother and sister in Christ. He hears their correction and humbly accepts it.
   - The result in both situations is that the word of God continues to be taught and people hear the truth (v 11, 27-28).

7. **In what settings are you most likely to be held back from speaking and acting in accordance with the truth? How can we make sure God's word wins?**
   Try to help the group to see how fear, lack of understanding, and sin (such

as lack of humility) can obscure the truth. How do these things prevent us from sharing the good news with non-Christians, and from supporting other Christians to grow in Christ-likeness? We should seek help in the same places that Paul and Apollos found it. As we pray and read God's Spirit-inspired Bible, God's own words will spur us on and help us to understand the truth. We also have a duty to kindly correct our Christian brothers and sisters when we see them going astray.

8. **Luke describes the group Paul speaks to in Ephesus as "disciples." But what is lacking, and how serious is that lack?**
   These men are "disciples" but not yet Christians. They hold to an "almost Christianity": they have not received the Holy Spirit, because they do not realize that salvation comes only through Jesus Christ. Paul shows them that they have not understood John's baptism, which pointed toward the baptism of faith in Jesus. His message proves effective as they confess Jesus as Lord and show outward signs that confirm their inward spiritual change.

9. **Why do you think Luke tells us the value of the books burned in verse 19?**
   The value of what they burned testified to the power of the gospel and the preached word of God. The idolatry of Ephesus ended up in an ash heap.

   - **How does this event help us to understand what repentance is?**
     This is a demonstration of the nature of true repentance: it is both costly and public.

10. **Compare verses 1-7, 8-10, and 11-20. Very different things happen in each of these passages. But what is consistent about Paul's behavior?**
    Throughout these verses we see how the message of Christianity spread—through the faithful, persistent preaching of God's word. Paul summons all to repent and believe. He continues to do this regardless of what happens, knowing that all will be held to account for their response to the gospel.

11. **Of all the signs we have seen of the strength of the word of the Lord and the name of Jesus in Ephesus, which do you think is the clearest?**
    The group could discuss any of the following:
    - The correction of Apollos and the strength of his preaching
    - The baptism of the twelve disciples and their new ability to speak in tongues and prophesy
    - The spread of the word from one building to the whole of the province of Asia
    - The miracles done by God through Paul
    - The fear shown by the residents of Ephesus after the sons of Sceva are humiliated

- The conviction of sin and costly repentance of those who practiced magic arts

12. **Look back across chapter 19. Why is it a problem when as Christians we forget to think and talk about...**
   - **Jesus' power and his promise of blessing?**
   The men in verses 1-7 want to follow God but have not understood the power of Jesus. They receive the Holy Spirit and then the transformative power of the gospel is seen in them. Without the Spirit we cannot be saved and transformed.
   - **the cost and pain of repentance and discipleship?**
   Like the sons of Sceva, many in our day invoke Jesus without really knowing him. They want a Jesus they can use—a spiritual talisman, not a Jesus who saves and who commands us to follow him. If we present Christianity simply as a life of peace and blessing, we have lost sight of the biblical expectations of Christian living. Following Christ means denying ourselves and taking up our cross.
   - **Which do you think your church is more likely to under- or over-emphasize?**
   Think about your own group as well as about the church as a whole. What can you do to make sure you are faithful to the truth?

5

The God Worth Serving

Acts 19:21 - 20:38

The Big Idea

God alone is worthy of worship, and everything we do should show that—our words, our plans, and our attitude to others.

Summary

Paul now makes plans to go to Jerusalem and then Rome (Acts 19:21-22). But while he is still in Ephesus, a seismic disturbance shakes things up (v 23-34). Demetrius the silversmith is losing business because the spreading of the gospel has led to fewer people buying his pagan shrines. He feels it necessary to rise up and make a public push against Christianity, provoking a violent riot. We see how deeply subversive the gospel is here, as it confronts pagan religion, the economy, and the whole way of life. Finally, however, the town clerk shows up to restore order and peace (v 35-41).

Paul departs, utilizing his travels to encourage the churches in many regions (20:1-6). In Troas we see the first mention in the New Testament of Christian worship on the first day of the week—what we call Sunday (v 7-12). The Christians gather in the evening, and when the clock strikes midnight, Paul's preaching does not cease. But his preaching is interrupted by a miracle. One listener, balanced on a window ledge, falls asleep and plummets to his untimely demise. Paul bends over the young man and raises him to life by the power of God. Then he goes on preaching. The word of God stands as the centerpiece of Paul's ministry.

Paul goes on toward Jerusalem (v 13-16). The time has come for him to say his farewell to the Ephesians. He calls their elders to Miletus, some 80 kilometers (50 miles) from Ephesus (v 17). This is the result of his strategic, Christ-centred impulse. He knows that he doesn't have time to visit Ephesus if he wants to make it to Jerusalem by Pentecost. He also seeks to disengage himself from direct oversight of the Ephesian church; they must be self-sufficient.

In his farewell speech, we see the character of Paul's legacy. He reminds the elders about his faithful ministry among them (v 18-27). Knowing that he will never see them again, he also charges them to persevere in the ministry with the same boldness that he showed (v 28-32). He shows that powerful ministries which effect real and glorious change flow from men and women who possess a single-minded and passionate love for God and his glory. Paul concludes with a final defense of his ministry (v 33-35) and says farewell. Luke intends to capture the emotion of Paul's departure as he kneels with the elders and prays with them (v 36-38). His impact on this church's life cannot be overstated.

Optional Extra

Test your group's knowledge of the 1st-century Gentile world with a short quiz. Correct answers are in *italics*!

1. What was the Roman name for the Greek god Zeus? Apollo, *Jupiter*, or Thor?
2. How long did it take to build the Temple of Artemis in Ephesus? 8 months, 50 years, or *120 years*?
3. How many gods did the ancient Greeks and Romans believe in? Nine, twelve, or *unlimited numbers of gods*?
4. When did Ephesus come under Roman rule? *133 BC*, 31 BC, or AD 6?
5. What was the main way in which pagan gods were worshiped? Singing, *sacrifices*, or moral living?
6. What did they use to make statues of gods and goddesses? Stone, bronze, ivory, or *all of the above*?
7. What did people ask the god Asclepius for? *Physical healing*, good weather, or financial prosperity?
8. Where did people worship gods? In temples, in roadside shrines, at home, or *all of the above*?
9. Alexander the Great started off as ruler of Macedonia in 336 BC and expanded

his territory south and east. Where was the furthest place he conquered? *Pakistan*, southern France, Morocco, or all of the above?

10. What famous ancient city was situated not far from Troas? Alexandria, *Troy*, or Carthage?

Guidance for Questions

1. **What kinds of things are people proud of? How do they show their pride?**
   The aim of this question is to start thinking about what people worship and how they show that. Perhaps it will be something physical, such as sports facilities or public buildings. Perhaps it will be an institution, such as a sports team or a good school. Perhaps it will be people-related: family or long-standing friendships or the way strangers are welcomed locally. Perhaps it will be more personal achievements, such as financial gains or house improvements. They might show their pride by treating things or people particularly well, or by being hostile to those who oppose or (they believe) disgrace them. They might have pictures or wear clothes that express their loyalty.

2. **Why is Demetrius worried about what Paul is saying (v 24-27)?**
   The silversmith is losing business. Paul understands that God is one, so he claims that any other god is in fact no god at all. He persuades people away from the worship of Artemis. Demetrius knows that if Paul continues to persuade others, the craftsmen will be out of business and Artemis will be forsaken (v 27).

3. **Compare the reaction of the crowds (v 28-34) to that of the town clerk (v 35-41). What is their attitude toward Artemis?**
   The crowd repeatedly chants, "Great is Artemis" (v 28, 34). They don't want to let go of their pagan worldview. The clerk, too, is clear that Artemis and her city are great (v 35-36).

- **Why do they respond differently to the Christian message?**
  Hysteria breaks out in the city and the crowd responds with violence. The fear shown by Paul's friends in v 30-31 shows us the danger from the mob. But they do not really know why they are angry (v 32). They don't want to hear the message at all (v 34). The town clerk, meanwhile, wants to bring order to the situation and defuse the conflict. He is more aware of what started the riot (v 38). He declares the Christians innocent of a two-part charge (v 37). The first concerns robbing the temple (being "sacrilegious"). The second is about blaspheming the goddess. But this second charge is more or less what the Christians have been doing (v 26). Either the clerk does not fully understand the Christian message, or he does understand but decides that the riot is more worrying than the blasphemy of his goddess.

4. **What is Paul's priority in all of this?**

   Paul has confronted the issue of idolatry and the pagan worldview head-on (v 26). In the riot he wants to go to defend himself, his friends, and his gospel (v 30), despite danger.

5. **Demetrius, the crowds, and the town clerk all say that Artemis is great. But what else do you think lies behind their actions? What desires fuel their worship of the goddess?**

   Demetrius is motivated by money; he is losing business. The crowds are either just angry for the sake of being angry or motivated by pride in their city. The town clerk represents the civic authority and prioritizes law and order.

- **How does that compare with what drives Paul?**

  Paul simply wants to preach the gospel and defend other believers. His devotion to God is not compromised by selfish motives.

6. **Think about the people you know and how their words and actions show what they really desire and worship. What do they daydream about, get excited about, prioritize, or fear?**

   Modern Westerners worship ideas, ambition, or power as objects of idolatry, just like the people of Ephesus. People today may be motivated by wealth and prosperity or a sense of pride in a particular place or an institution that represents it, such as a sports team. They may have their own moral principles, like the town clerk who prioritizes law and order. They may prioritize romantic or family relationships above all else. Christians can run the risk of allowing secular worldviews to pervert true Christian living. We must recognize when we are taking something less than God and rendering to it worship, of which only God is worthy.

7. **What do you think the believers think of the power Paul shows?**

   God's divine power manifests itself in splendor when the young man comes back to life. This is not a common occurrence! There are only seven cases in the whole Bible, apart from the resurrection of Jesus and the resurrections accompanying his death, where human beings are raised from the dead. Elijah and Elisha both do it by God's power (1 Kings 17:21-22; 2 Kings 4:34-35); Jesus raises Jairus' daughter (Mark 5:39-42), the young man of Nain (Luke 7:14-17), and Lazarus (John 11:43-44); Peter raises Dorcas (Acts 9:40), and Paul raises Eutychus.

- **Does it seem more or less important than his teaching?**

  Paul's focus is on the proclamation of the gospel; he carries on speaking (v 11). The word of God is the centerpiece of Paul's ministry. The miracle validates the message. If you have time, look up Luke 7:11-17 and 1 Kings 17:22-24 to see how this pattern is shown elsewhere too.

8. **In verses 1-6 and 13-16 we are given lots of details about Paul's journeys. Look back at 19:21. What shapes Paul's plans?**
Paul is directed by the Spirit. He wants ultimately to go to Rome, the center of the Gentile universe. He also wants to travel through Macedonia and Greece to strengthen the believers. He hopes to return to Jerusalem before the spring so that he can present his collection of money to the struggling church there.

9. **In verses 18-27, how does Paul describe the character of his work in Ephesus?**
   - He has served the Lord in humility (v 19), not for his own fame but for the sake of his hearers (v 20) and as a result of the call of God (v 24).
   - He has taught the word of God boldly, both in public and in private (v 20, 27).
   - He has preached repentance and faith to all (v 21).

- **In verses 33-35, how else does he say he has acted, and why?**
Paul didn't preach this gospel for selfish gain or ambition but for the glory of God. So he worked for his own money, both to avoid burdening others and to be able to show love in generosity to the needy.

Explore More

- ***Read 1 Corinthians 9:3-18. What does Paul say he has a right to?***
Paul has the right to eat and drink (v 4), to be accompanied by a wife (v 5), and to receive financial support from the churches he has planted (v 11-12, 14) so that he can spend all his time on gospel ministry.

- ***Why does he give up those rights?***
Paul recognizes that insisting on his own rights would mean hindering the gospel (v 12). He is completely driven by a desire to preach the gospel (v 16) and wants to make sure it is free of charge (v 18).

10. **In verses 28-32, how does Paul urge the Ephesian elders to lead the church well?**
    - Paul evokes Jesus' own self-description as the good shepherd. The Ephesian elders bear responsibility for King Jesus' flock; it is God who has given them this position (v 28).
    - Paul heightens the charge with the reminder that the sheep cost Jesus his very life (v 28).
    - He speaks about external threats to the church as "fierce wolves" (v 29), indicating their malevolent, murderous intent.
    - He mentions the internal threat of false teaching, which works more subtly to lead the sheep astray (v 30). Therefore the shepherds must "pay careful attention" (v 28) and "be alert" (v 31).
    - He reminds them of his own example of tirelessness and compassion (v 31).

- He tells them that they will be supported and saved by God, his word, and his grace (v 32).

11. **What does Paul's plan to go to Jerusalem tell us about his attitude toward his life?**
Paul knows that there will be significant danger in Jerusalem. But he also knows that God wants him to go there (v 22). He understands his position before the eternal God: a servant. He measures the worth of his life by whatever purpose God will use it for (v 24). He is controlled by one reality: the glory of God.

12. **How can we use our lives to display the fact that God alone is worthy of worship...**
   - **in what we say?**
   As in the gathering in verses 7-12, we should build our ministry around the preached word. Like Paul, we should not leave anything out of the gospel message, and we should never be afraid to speak about God (v 27).
   - **in how we plan?**
   Like Paul in verses 16-17, we should know our limits: there is not time for everything. The work of Christ reigns supreme, and Christians should rely on one another, not thinking of ourselves as indispensable. Like Paul, we should prioritize serving the Lord. Listening to God's word in Scripture with the help of the Holy Spirit will help us to be obedient in our planning.
   - **in how we treat others?**
   Christian ministry must be about people, bringing them to Christ and strengthening them in faith. We should display tender self-sacrificial love and humility, never being motivated by selfish gain or ambition. Leaders should develop other leaders rather than building their ministry around themselves.

6

Accused in Jerusalem

Acts 21:1 - 23:35

The Big Idea

God works both in our circumstances and through our faithful obedience to open doors for the gospel.

Summary

Paul's ministry now takes on a different character. The beginning of Acts 21 concludes his third missionary journey and begins the final phase of his life. Paul begins his new ministry of defending his faith while on trial. Our study will focus on what Paul says and does, and will spend less time looking at how others respond to him.

Luke continues to describe Paul's journey to Jerusalem (21:1-15). Along the way, he visits Christians who try to persuade him not to go to Jerusalem. But he declares his intention to press on toward certain persecution. His chief purpose centers on the proclamation of the gospel of God, whatever the cost.

In Jerusalem, the Christian leaders welcome Paul and his traveling companions, and Paul takes them through a travelogue from his latest journey (v 17-19). The elders respond by glorifying God for the ministry to the Gentiles (v 20). However, they are concerned about how other Jewish Christians will receive Paul. To maintain unity, they ask him to sponsor the purification of four men under the Nazirite vow (a sign of special dedication to the Lord: see Numbers 6:1-21), in order to deflect any charge of opposing the law (Acts 21:20-26). Paul humbly submits himself to their request, but non-believing Jews nevertheless stir up a mob to attack him with false accusations (v 27-30).

The crowd is calmed by the tribune, a military commander, who allows Paul to speak to the mob (v 31-40). In 22:1-21 we hear his speech, in which he uses the story of his life to declare that Jesus is God and that Gentiles, too, can be part of God's family. At this the mob returns to violent anarchy (v 22-23).

Paul is escorted away by the tribune, but he is still in trouble as he is tied up to be whipped (v 23-24). However, he stops the persecutors in their tracks by using his status as a Roman citizen to protect himself (v 25-29).

In chapter 23 we continue to see how God uses Paul's circumstances to enable him to preach the gospel in Jerusalem and ultimately be taken to Rome. First he is on trial before the chief priests (v 1-10), who end up being interrogated themselves by the gospel, thanks to Paul's masterful redirection of proceedings. Next, after God visits the apostle with words of comfort overnight (v 11), a plot against Paul leads to his being taken to the Roman governor. There is a serious conspiracy to kill him (v 12-15), which the tribune hears about (v 16-22). Recognizing that he must get Paul out of Jerusalem before he's murdered, the tribune hatches a plan to get Paul to Felix, the governor, in Caesarea (v 23-35). Paul is escorted out of Jerusalem by armed guards. God's plan, despite enormous persecution, is falling into place.

Optional Extra

Ask some group members to share three-minute testimonies (either of how they became a Christian or of a particular time when God worked clearly in their lives): one minute on life before that moment, one on how God changed them, and one on life since then. How has God used the circumstances of their lives to bring them to him?

Guidance for Questions

1. **Can you think of specific times of difficulty in your life when God has helped you to be faithful to him and has worked through you to impact others?**
Encourage group members to talk specifically about how God has helped them—through his word, by his Spirit, using other people—as well as what faithfulness looks like in different situations. How might their acting and speaking faithfully in the face of opposition or other pressures have impacted those around them—both Christians and non-Christians?

2. **How does Paul feel about committing himself to his decision to go (v 13)?**
Paul is fully aware of the impending suffering, and he says he is "ready." He does not hesitate to continue on his mission. At the same time, he says that the other believers are breaking his heart.

3. **Why are the elders of the Jewish church worried about what people think of Paul?**
The Jewish believer cannot find salvation in the Jewish traditions. At the same time, Scripture does not forbid Jews to continue Jewish customs. It seems that many feel strongly about these customs, although they know that they are saved through Christ alone. But the elders are concerned that Jewish Christians have misunderstood Paul's teaching on this issue, believing that he rejects the Law of Moses altogether (v 21). They are worried that this could lead to a fissure in the already fragile bonds between Jewish and Gentile Christians.

- **What solution do they suggest to him?**
They ask Paul to sponsor the purification of four men under a vow. This is a Jewish custom, and by taking part in it, Paul should be able to deflect any charge of opposing the Law of Moses.

4. **What is Paul accused of (21:28-29, 38)?**
   - Non-believing Jews accuse Paul of being against the law and the temple, and of bringing a Gentile into the inner sanctuary of the temple, which was off-limits to non-Jews.
   - The tribune assumes that Paul is an Egyptian who in AD 54 led a revolt in Jerusalem.

5. **Acts 22:22 tells us that, until that point, the crowd listened to Paul. If you were a Jewish member of the crowd, what might you be thinking...**

- **by the end of verse 5?**
If Paul were to stop his speech at this point, the crowd would applaud. He has turned his mind to winning over the Jewish crowd by describing his Jewish background: speaking the Hebrew language (21:40), addressing the crowd respectfully (22:1), expressing his Jewish identity in his home

town, his education, and his zeal for the law (v 3), and describing his persecution of Christians as an example of that zeal (v 4-5).

- **by the end of verse 16?**
  Next Paul tells of his conversion (also told in Acts 9). He continues to show his Jewish credentials, talking about Ananias, a devout Jew, who told him that the God he had studied under Gamaliel was the same God he had encountered on the road to Damascus (v 12-16). But Paul has changed his tone, declaring that Jesus is God (v 8, 10, 14). Luke does not record a response from the Jewish crowds. They do not react aggressively, perhaps because he has not said anything yet to make their accusations against him credible. That is what they are listening out for.

- **by the end of verse 21?**
  After Paul announces that the Gentiles are fellow recipients of the gospel, the mob returns to violent anarchy.

6. **In what ways might the gospel message be offensive in our culture?**
   It remains tempting to shape God to the culture, rather than summoning the culture to turn to God. Try to get the group to think about some of the messages and values they hear every day. How is the gospel different from those? Ask group members to share times when people have been offended by their faith.

7. **How can you make sure you remain faithful and put God first as you interact with others?**
   We need to think about how the gospel offends the assumptions and values of any society so that we are prepared to challenge the culture when the gospel does offend. Like Paul, we must guard against trying to make the gospel seem less offensive than it is.

8. **How does Paul take advantage of his background for the sake of the gospel...**

- **in 22:25-30?**
  Paul uses his citizenship as a protection. He tells the tribune that he is about to illegally torture a Roman citizen. Paul would endure any suffering which befell him, but he does not pursue unnecessary suffering. He uses his citizenship as a gift of God in order to continue to advance the gospel.

- **in 23:6-10?**
  Paul recognized the makeup of his audience: half were Sadducees, who denied a bodily resurrection, and half Pharisees, who believed in a resurrection from the dead. Paul leverages this disparity and his own background as a Pharisee. He redirects the attention from himself to a significant doctrinal matter. The disagreement culminates in the Pharisee party declaring Paul innocent of all charges. The scene ends with the tribune intervening to remove Paul.

9. **In 23:1-5, why does Paul speak angrily to the high priest?**
   Luke does not offer a judgment on Paul's words. We could say that Paul lost his temper, and this is behavior we should not seek to emulate. On the other hand, Jesus used similar language against Jewish leaders in Matthew 23:27. Paul's anger is not based on the physical hurt he has sustained but on Ananias' contravention of the Old Testament law.

   - **Why does he apologize?**
   Paul grounds his confession not in the character of Ananias but in the Old Testament Scriptures: it is wrong to speak evil of a ruler. This demonstrates that his good conscience is directed by God, not men.

10. **Why does the tribune say that he is sending Paul to the Roman governor (v 26-30)?**
    - Paul is a Roman citizen (v 27).
    - Paul has done nothing to deserve death or imprisonment (v 29).
    - There has been a plot against him, from which he needed to be rescued (v 30).

    Notice too what the tribune leaves out of his letter. He is a self-preserving bureaucrat and does not reveal the whole truth: that he has had Paul arrested and almost flogged, in violation of his rights as a Roman citizen. Luke contrasts the self-serving soldier and his half-truthful letter with the Christ-exalting apostle and his fully truthful testimony.

11. **Look back at verse 11. God speaks directly to Paul to outline his plans for him: to testify about him in Jerusalem and in Rome. Across all the passages in this study, what different things have contributed to the fulfillment of these plans?**
    - *Paul's obedience in going to Jerusalem.* Paul's persistence and sense of urgency, seen in 20:16, results eventually in the opportunity to declare the gospel directly to powerful Jewish leaders.
    - *Paul's background and history.* We can deduce the providential hand of God over Paul's status as a Roman citizen, allowing him the protections of the empire. Meanwhile, his Jewish background wins him a hearing before the crowds (22:2).
    - *Paul's faithfulness to the truth.* He does not miss out points which elicit hostility and mockery from the crowds. He tells the whole truth about the gospel and his own mission.
    - *Paul's wisdom at the chief priests' council.* He carefully shifts the focus of the trial to the key doctrine of resurrection, exposing the hearts and worldviews of those he is speaking to.
    - *The plot against Paul.* The Jewish plot did not surprise God. Before they even hatched their plot, he confounded their efforts. He uses the plot to cause the tribune to send Paul to the Roman governor. Paul is smuggled out of Jerusalem with 470 soldiers to protect him!

12. **How do we expect God to use us? Can you think of ways in which God could use...**
    - **your present circumstances (even if they seem bad)?**
    Like Paul, we can reflect on our lives and know the power of our story as it demonstrates the transformative grace of the gospel. Encourage group members to consider how God might be transforming them or protecting them through their current circumstances, or who they have opportunities to reach at the moment.
    - **your faithful obedience in those circumstances?**
    The question should not be "Why does suffering happen to me?" but rather "How can I proclaim the gospel of Jesus in the midst of my trials?" How can we make sure that we are culturally distinct? How can we turn conversations toward God? What impact could that have?

7

Hope on Trial

Acts 24:1 - 26:32

The Big Idea

Our hope in the resurrection and the way we live complement one another. Holy living bears witness to the transformation brought by Jesus and should give us opportunities to speak about the hope that we have.

Summary

In chapter 24, the high priest comes to see Felix, the governor, to make the case against Paul with false accusations (v 1-9). But when Felix gives Paul the opportunity to respond, Paul dismantles each accusation (v 10-21). He asserts his innocence and declares his hope in the resurrection of the dead.

Felix knows enough about Christianity to know that Ananias' accusations are baseless (v 22). From this point onward, the Jews have nothing on Paul. The case simply becomes a matter of the Roman judicial process—exactly as God intended. Felix and his wife listen to Paul and show an interest in Christianity but fail to repent, and he remains in custody (v 23-27).

Acts 25 introduces Felix's successor, Festus, who immediately heads to Jerusalem to try to establish a relationship with the Jews. They urgently present their accusations against Paul, but Festus does not turn him over to them (v 1-5). Back in Caesarea, Paul insists that he has nothing to hide and appeals to Caesar (v 6-12). Festus agrees: Paul will go and stand before the emperor of Rome.

First, however, Festus recounts the case to Agrippa, the king (v 13-27). He perceives that the heart of the matter surrounds this man Jesus, who Paul believes has risen from the grave. He notes that Paul has done nothing to deserve death and asks for help in defining the charges against him.

Chapter 26 contains Paul's defense before King Agrippa (v 1-23). He tells his testimony, which both contains the truth of Christ and shows his grace as it has worked on Paul. He recounts his life as a persecutor of Christians (v 4-12) and retells his conversion and his commissioning to become a missionary, evangelist, and theologian (v 13-18). He details how he has obeyed this commission (v 19-22) and announces that his message is founded on the prophets, the text of the Old Testament (v 22-23).

When Paul mentions the resurrection, Festus charges him with insanity (v 24). But Paul makes a final appeal to Agrippa and then to the whole audience (v 25-29). He does not seek release for himself but that they may repent and believe the gospel. The chapter ends with the authorities agreeing that Paul is innocent; yet they have no choice but to send him to Rome (v 30-32).

Optional Extra

Give everyone a different story, object or concept, and ask them to explain it in just three words, without using the original word itself. Everyone else must guess what it is they are trying to explain. Think of your own or try these: *Christmas; computer; pencil; Cinderella; brick; jigsaw puzzle; Harry Potter; flu; happiness.*

Guidance to Questions

1. **How would you sum up the gospel in three words?**
   Give everyone time to think of their three words; then ask them all to share. The point is not necessarily to give the perfect explanation but to practice being succinct. Some may emphasize the story of what Jesus did (e.g. "Jesus is alive"). Others may focus on the result of what he did (e.g. "Jesus saves sinners" or "Jesus forgives me"). As we will see, Paul speaks clearly both about what he believes and about how that has changed his own life.

2. **What tactics does Tertullus use to try to persuade Felix?**
   - v 2-3: Tertullus constructs his opening lines to shamefully flatter the Roman governor.
   - v 4-6: He makes three statements of false accusation against Paul. First, he describes him as a seditious plague on the region, threatening stability. Second, he charges him with being the leader of a sect, a fanatical political party. Third, he claims that he is guilty of temple desecration. It is this charge which could afford the Jews the opportunity to execute Paul.
   - v 8: He hopes to bring Paul under the direct examination of the

governor, believing that Paul will falter and his case will be won.

3. **How does Paul dismantle each of Tertullus' accusations?**
   - Paul mentions the mere twelve days he has been in Jerusalem, ridiculing Tertullus' claim that he has been stirring up dissension (v 11), and insists that the Jews found him in no disputes with any person in Jerusalem (v 12).
   - Paul testifies to Christianity, the roots of which he firmly grounds in the Jewish Scriptures (v 14). Far from being a political sect, he claims that Christians are committed to following the way of the Lord—a way of spiritual reform, not political subversion.
   - He challenges the Jewish leaders to explain what they think he has done in violation of Jewish customs (v 18-19).

4. **Why is it important that Paul's conscience is clean (v 15-16)?**
   Unlike his opponents, Paul locks his eyes on eternity. Jesus' resurrection from the dead (v 15), coming as the first of many in the eternal family of God, is fundamental to Christianity. It establishes both the hope of repentant sinners and the despair of the unrepentant. Paul knows that he will one day stand before God to give an account for his life and conduct. He can say that his conscience is clean because he always strives to fear God rather than men.

Explore More

- ***Read 1 Peter 3:14-17. Where in Acts 24 can you see Paul acting according to this advice?***
- ***"Have no fear of them, nor be troubled"***
  v 10: Paul does not flatter Felix but makes his defense cheerfully and with integrity.
- ***"In your hearts honor Christ the Lord as holy"***
  v 14-16: Paul operates out of a fear of God.
- ***"Always being prepared to make a defense to anyone who asks you for a reason for the hope that is in you"***
  v 14-16: Paul roots his identity as a Christian in the Old Testament, which contains the promise from God to his people of the coming day of his Son.
  v 21: He repeats his hope in the resurrection of the dead.
- ***"Do it with gentleness and respect"***
  v 10: He speaks respectfully to Felix, simply stating the facts about his rule.
- ***"Having a good conscience"***
  Throughout, Paul asserts his innocence clearly, recognizing that God is his judge.

5. **Look at how Felix and then Festus respond to Paul. What are their reasons for treating him as they do?**
   Felix and Festus both want to secure their own version of peace and prosperity. They both realize

that Paul is innocent and treat him respectfully. But their hearts are hard to his message.

- 24:22-23: Felix has a good working knowledge of Christianity. He knows enough to know that Ananias has come with baseless accusations. He therefore gives Paul a considerable measure of freedom; he is kept in custody, not necessarily as a criminal but for his own protection.
- v 24-25: As Paul preaches the true tenets of the Christian faith, Felix is struck to the core and filled with fear at the thought of his coming judgment. But rather than repenting and trusting in Christ, Felix dismisses Paul.
- v 26: Felix continues to hear Paul, but he does not listen to his message; he is motivated by money. He is blind to the gospel.
- v 27: He leaves Paul in prison because of the Jews, operating out of an unhealthy fear of man.
- 25:1-9: Festus likewise wants to establish a good relationship with the Jews, but because of Paul's Roman citizenship, he does not just hand him over but gives him a formal trial.
- v 10-12: Festus recognizes Paul's innocence. But he does not give a verdict.

6. **Why is Festus at a loss about Paul?**
   Festus almost certainly expected the Jews to accuse Paul of egregious acts against both the Jews and Rome (v 18). You can almost sense the puzzled tone in Festus' voice as he relays to Agrippa the fact that the heart of the matter surrounds this man named Jesus, whom Paul believed to have risen from the grave (v 19). He cannot understand the resurrection; people do not come back to life. He therefore asks Agrippa for help in defining the charges against Paul (v 26-27).

7. **How do people nowadays respond to the message of Jesus' resurrection from the dead, and why?**
   Some, like Felix and Drusilla, are entrenched in lives of sin and disobedience, and are scandalized by the idea of coming judgment. Others think that the claim of the resurrection is mad because people do not rise from the dead.

- **How can we prepare ourselves for these responses?**
  The gospel of Jesus Christ is a beautiful scandal that ought to be shared with unbounded passion, whatever the consequences. Like Paul, we must remember that it is God before whom we will one day stand to give an account for our lives. We can also follow Paul's example in using rational explanations to support our claim, especially using the Old Testament to explain the promise of God to his people.

8. **How does Paul explain the truth of the gospel?**
   It may be helpful to split the group into four, giving each sub-group one

of the following passages to look at.

- v 6-8: Paul believes that Jesus rose from the dead. He shows that the Hebrew Scriptures point to such a resurrection.
- v 15-18: Paul describes Jesus' mission. People are spiritually blind, and their eyes can only be opened by Christ. Wandering in blindness is not morally neutral but means serving Satan, and he can only be defeated by Christ. By faith people will receive forgiveness of sins and an eternal place in the household of God.
- v 19-20: Paul describes his message. He understands the gospel as not only good news but a summons to repentance. We must turn away from sin and pursue Christ.
- v 22-23: Paul says that he has proclaimed exactly what the prophets predicted: God's redemptive plan spans the ages. The entire Old Testament points to the coming of God's Messiah, who would not only suffer but die; and not only die but be raised from the grave.

9. How does Paul show the transformative power of the gospel in his own life?

- v 9-12: Paul recounts his life as a persecutor of Christians and his hatred for the message of the gospel. He shows that he was once like those Jews who now condemn him and ridicule his beliefs.
- v 13-18: Paul tells his hearers what happened to radically alter his course. One minute, he was setting out to persecute the people of God. The next minute, he belonged to that very family.
- v 14: God's providential hand over the entire span of Paul's life is revealed. A goad is a sharp stick used by a plowman to prod a sluggish ox into moving faster. Jesus' phrase shows that he had been prodding Paul toward himself throughout his life.
- v 19-21: Paul frames his mission as a matter of obedience, and describes how his fidelity to his gospel conviction has driven him from region to region, proclaiming the faith he received on the Damascus road.

10. How does Paul's own story exemplify his evangelistic message in verses 18 and 23?

- Paul's immediate radical conversion shows how God is the one who opens eyes; the moment we place our faith in Christ, he delivers us from the domain of darkness and transfers us into the kingdom of his beloved Son (Colossians 1:13).
- Paul's transformation from persecutor to missionary gives an example of repentance and "deeds in keeping with repentance" (Acts 26:20).

11. Why does Paul think he is in a better situation than his audience (v 29)?

Paul sees right through the pomp and prosperity of the king and the governor. Even though he is in chains, he still has the eternal riches of Christ, which eclipse all the wealth, power, and comfort this world can offer.

- **Do Festus, Agrippa, and Bernice understand that?**
  No. Festus has charged him with insanity (v 24), and Agrippa has avoided Paul's call to repentance (v 28). In verses 31-32 they confer with one another, recognizing Paul's innocence. They don't understand why he has appealed to Caesar, when he would otherwise be released.

12. In what ways and situations could you proclaim the hope that you have?
Remind group members of their three-word summaries of the gospel at the beginning of the study. Based on how Paul gives reasons for his hope in the resurrection, would they change their three words? Can you think of different situations in which you might share the good news, and what you might say to explain it?

- **How could the way you live bear witness to this hope?**
  As we summon others to repentance, we must live holy lives ourselves. This does not remove the possibility that we will be accused of wickedness; the darkness hates the light. 1 Peter 2:12 reminds believers of the hope of obedience. God will receive glory from our good deeds today as they show accusations to be false; and on the Day of Judgment he will vindicate his people.

8

Calm in the Storm

Acts 27:1 - 28:31

The Big Idea

God's sovereign will can never be thwarted. When we find ourselves in difficulties, trusting in him will give us a calm confidence as we continue to proclaim the hope of the gospel.

Summary

Acts 27 ushers in a climactic demonstration of God's providence and sovereignty. Paul faces very arduous situations, yet readers quite clearly see that he is right where God wants him.

Now a political prisoner, Paul embarks on a journey across the Mediterranean Sea (v 1). The journey takes place in the fall, which presents a grave threat to the safety of the travellers, and forces the ship to divert (v 2-8). Paul urges the centurion not to press on, but his advice is ignored (v 9-12). The ship is pushed out into the open sea, and the sailors become desperate (v 13-20). Yet Paul enjoins them not to give up, exuding an unyielding confidence in God's sovereign will; God has promised to take Paul to Rome, and he will (v 21-26). Paul no longer speaks like a prisoner, and the sailors place their trust in him as he continues to advise and encourage them (v 27-38).

When the ship eventually runs aground, the centurion is determined to save Paul, and all are brought to land, as God promised (v 39-44). The whole chapter presents us with a remarkable picture of God's sovereignty and power.

The final chapter of Acts concludes the book on a similar note of God's providential care for his apostle and the spread of the gospel. The travelers have made it to the island of Malta, where they are shown extraordinary kindness (v 1-2). Paul performs miracles on the island, and the people there honor him (v 3-10).

In the spring the voyagers set sail again and finally arrive in Rome, where many come to greet Paul and encourage him in the task that lies before him (v 11-15). Paul seeks not a defense attorney but the local Jewish leaders—inviting them to the house where he is being guarded—and speaks to them, summarizing his story, professing his innocence, and boldly stating the hope of the gospel (v 16-20).

The Jews listen but are divided over his message (v 21-24). Eventually Paul loses his audience, after proclaiming a prophetic word from Isaiah indicating that even after he preached, the people would not listen (v 25-28). Paul continues to live and preach in Rome for two years (v 30-31), doing exactly what God wants. We are left looking forward, facing a task unfinished, and recognizing that God is still moving in and through his church.

Optional Extra

Ask everyone to anonymously write down a fear that they or someone else might have (e.g. fear of public speaking, fear of spiders, fear of failure). Fold them up and gather them into a bowl. Each group member must take a piece of paper out of the bowl. They must read out the fear and describe who or what could help: who can the person trust to overcome their fear? Then they must guess who wrote that fear down. Make the point that only God, and having the right attitude toward him, can ultimately drive out all fear.

Guidance for Questions

1. **What are some different ways in which people respond to difficulties?**
   Hardships can alter our behavior. Often they make us more stressed, more angry, or more fearful. They can cause rifts between people, or they can cause people to retreat into themselves. They also make people rethink their priorities and what they are living for. In this study we will see that Paul's response to difficulties is

calm trust. He is living for God, whose will cannot be thwarted.

2. **What is the centurion's view of Paul on this part of the journey?**
   Paul is escorted by a centurion from the Augustan Cohort, who were directly responsible for protecting Caesar. But he is not treated as a criminal. He is also accompanied by Luke—who indirectly includes himself as one of those on the journey, saying, "We put to sea"—and another friend, Aristarchus (v 2). In Sidon Paul is allowed to meet with other Christians (v 3). However, when Paul gives nautical advice, urging the centurion not to press on with the journey, he is heard but not followed (v 9-11).

3. **Look at what happens in verses 14-15, and how the sailors respond. How do the travelers feel by the end of verse 20?**
   They feel desperate. Phoenix seems to be the perfect winter harbor, but on the way there, a rushing north-easter wind causes them to lose control of the ship, and pushes it out into the open sea (v 14-15). The sailors' actions show us their despair:
   - v 16-17: They raise the lifeboat, which was usually towed behind the main vessel but could ram the ship in a storm.
   - v 17: They frap the ship, wrapping it with ropes and cables in an effort to hold it together and buy time before it sinks.
   - v 18: As a further precaution, they begin throwing the cargo overboard to lighten the ship—dumping their own livelihood to avoid sinking.
   - v 19: They are forced to throw out the ship's tackle. This means they can no longer control its direction or speed. They are simply giving themselves to the storm in the hopes of riding it out or being rescued.

   By verse 20 they have all, including Luke, lost hope.

4. **How does Paul seem to feel, and why?**
   Paul is calm. He reveals that an angel has instructed him to have no fear because God wills that he should testify before Caesar, and has also promised the safety of every soul on board the ship (v 23-24). Paul exudes an unyielding confidence in God's sovereign will, even when disaster looks certain.

- **How does this affect the way he behaves?**
  Paul does not become angry with God for the trials he is enduring but allows them to lead him into a greater dependence upon God. He witnesses to all those on board of the goodness and sovereign power of the one true God. He knows that he must act in accordance with God's will, directing the sailors to run the ship aground as an act of faith (v 26). Paul continues to direct the crew according to the revelation of God (v 30-32). Paul's trust in the providence of God makes him calm. As the ship cruises toward

certain wreckage, Paul advises the crew to sit, rest, and take a meal (v 33-36). He gives thanks to God (v 35), exemplifying trust, serenity, and gratitude.

5. **Trace the actions of the sailors and soldiers through the passage. How do you think their view of Paul—and his God—changes?**
   - v 27-30: The sailors, with their view obscured by darkness, believe that their ship is approaching an impending shoreline and begin to lower the lifeboats. They seek to escape from the ship.
   - v 31-32: However, the centurion has placed trust in Paul and cuts the ropes of the lifeboat to prevent anyone leaving the ship.
   - v 36: All the travelers are encouraged by Paul's words in verses 33-35, which no doubt have a profound impact and clear gospel witness. They abide by his instruction.
   - v 38: They continue to dump weight to make the inevitable impact less severe. Although encouraged by Paul, they are still aware of the danger.
   - v 39-41: They run the vessel aground, according to Paul's original instructions (v 26).
   - v 42: The soldiers know that if they go back to Rome without their prisoners, they will face the same judgment as the prisoners. So they devise a plan to kill them and then blame it on the extreme situation.
   - v 43-44: The centurion thwarts this mass murder as he has developed a trust in Paul.

6. **Look up Matthew 6:25-34; John 14:1-6; Romans 8:28-30; and Revelation 21:1-4. How could these passages help us to share Paul's calm trust in the providence of God?**

   Paul presses on because of God's promise. We too must not lose sight of the spectacular reward that awaits those who obey God. He has promised that we will be with him, face to face—that death will be no more and sin will pass away. God calls his people to seize his promises and hold them tight.

- **What impact could this have on those around us?**

  Like the Maltese people in the next passage, some may admire us for our trust in God. Others may follow our lead, like the centurion, and it may bring God glory by pointing them to his power at work. However, many will be less certain, like the sailors who try to escape from the ship.

7. **What does the snakebite incident show us...**

- **about Paul?**

  Unlike the Maltese people, Paul trusts the providence of God. He shakes off the snake as though nothing has happened. His composure is extraordinary.

- **about God?**

  Everyone believes Paul will soon die,

but their worldview must succumb to the prevailing, powerful, and sovereign glory of the true God. Indeed, Paul does not die.

8. **What encourages Paul on this part of the journey?**
    - v 13-14: He finds Christians at Puteoli and stays with them. How did Christianity make it there? We do not know. This reminds us that it is God himself who has powerfully advanced the gospel throughout the known world. The mission of the gospel rises above Paul or any other individual.
    - v 15: Christians from Rome come to greet Paul and encourage him in the task that lies before him. Their words help him to press on in faithful obedience.

9. **In verses 17-20, how does Paul explain his circumstances to the Jewish leaders?**
    Paul summarizes the reason why he has come to Rome as a prisoner, recounting the events in Jerusalem and asserting his innocence. He declares his allegiance to the people of Israel and the heritage of his nation, and boldly states that he possesses the hope of Israel. Paul says that this hope, which they share, has led to his chains.

10. **Why do the Jewish leaders respond in the way they do in verses 21-25?**
    The Jewish leaders initially want Paul to give an account of his message (v 22) but are divided over it (v 24). Eventually he loses his audience (v 25). Paul quotes from Isaiah 6:9-10, where God spoke to Isaiah indicating that even after he had preached, the people would not listen. Paul applies this prophetic judgment to the Jews in his crowd.

    - **Do you think Paul is disappointed by their response?**
    Paul mentions the Holy Spirit in verse 25 to ground the authority of his pronouncement not in himself but in God. He trusts God's plans. His speech ends with confidence: the Gentiles will listen and be saved. Just as it has in the narrative of Acts, the gospel will meet a positive response in the most surprising of places and from the most unlikely of people.

    - ***OPTIONAL: How do verses 24-28 fit in with Paul's experiences elsewhere?***
    Paul states that God has judged the Jews in his audience because they have turned from his gospel. This provides a conclusion for what we have seen throughout his missionary journeys: Paul's message is repeatedly rejected by Jews and accepted by Gentiles. The future of the church is with the Gentiles.

11. **Why do you think Luke ends the book so abruptly? What will happen next?**
    The conclusion leaves us exactly where the Holy Spirit wants us—ready for the "next chapter," which is still being written today. Luke ends

his narrative with an implied question: Peter preached the kingdom in Jerusalem, Philip proclaimed Christ in Samaria, and Paul announced Christ around the Roman Empire—where will you go?

12. **How would you sum up the message of Acts 13 – 28 in a sentence?** Give the group a little time to look back through previous chapters. The second half of Acts is not a biography of Paul but of the early church and its faithfulness in spreading the gospel to the ends of the earth. It chronicles a faithful God who keeps his promises, preserves his people, expands his message, and establishes an eternal people.

- **What has the Holy Spirit been challenging or encouraging you about in your own life as a result of reading this part of God's word?** Some group members may be able to share examples of how God has already been changing them as they have read Acts 13 – 28. Others may need to be encouraged to think more about how it applies to their lives. Try to make sure that everyone goes away with one challenge or encouragement to change.

thegoodbook COMPANY

BIBLICAL | RELEVANT | ACCESSIBLE

At The Good Book Company we are dedicated to helping Christians and local churches grow. We believe that God's growth process always starts with hearing clearly what he has said to us through his timeless and flawless word—the Bible.

Ever since we opened our doors in 1991, we have been striving to produce resources that are biblical, relevant, and accessible. By God's grace, we have grown to become an international publisher, encouraging ordinary Christians of every age and stage and every background and denomination to live for Christ day by day and equipping churches to grow in their knowledge of God, their love for one another, and the effectiveness of their outreach.

Call one of our friendly team for a discussion of your needs or visit one of our local websites for more information on the resources and services we provide.

Your friends at The Good Book Company